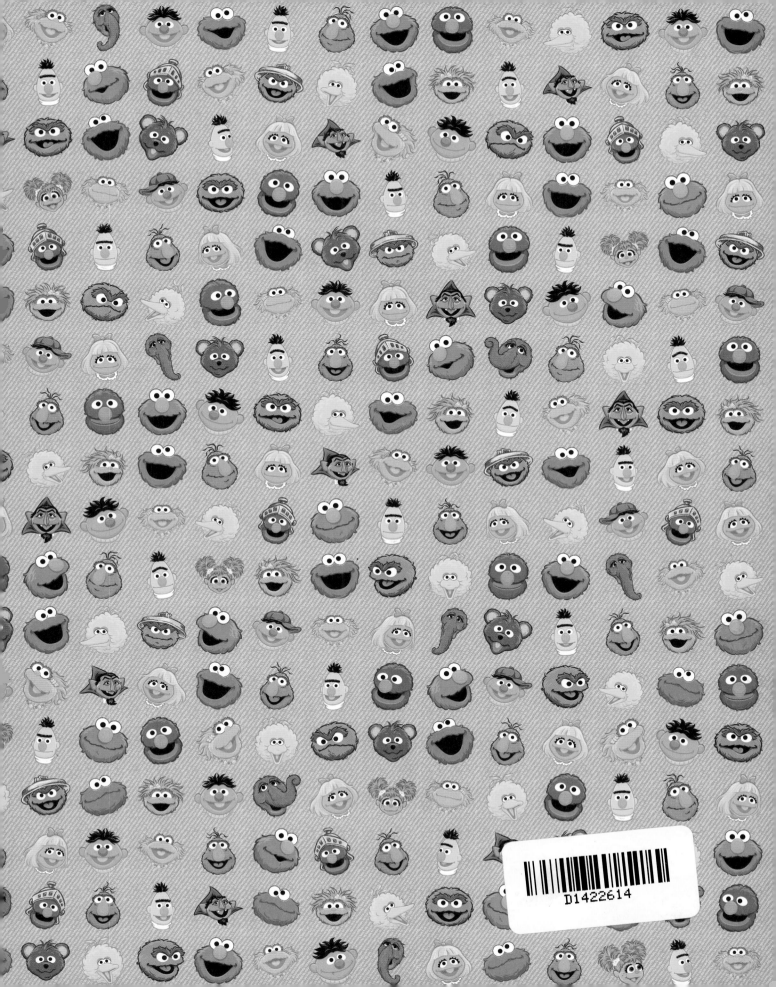

123 SESAME STREET®

BIG BOOK of Crafts

First published by Parragon in 2009

Parragon
Queen Street House
4 Queen Street
Bath BA1 1HE, UK

ISBN 978-1-4075-3810-5

Printed in China

123

SESAME STREET®

BIG BOOK OF Crafts

PaRragon

Bath · New York · Singapore · Hong Kong · Cologne · Delhi · Melbourne

Contents

This book is full of creative, fun things to make for your family, your friends and yourself for all kinds of occasions.

ELMO'S AWESOME ANIMALS

ZOES'S FUN WITH PAPER

OSCAR'S TOP TRASH CRAFTS

COOKIE MONSTER'S FUN FOOD

PRAIRIE DAWN'S GREAT GIFTS

BIG BIRD'S MARVELOUS MODELING

SNUFFY'S TOYS & GAMES

GROVER'S CELEBRATION CRAFTS

ABBY CADABBY'S GARDEN CRAFTS

Tips for Parents and Caregivers

This book is for the whole family. Its primary purpose is to bring together parents and children, from preschoolers to teens, to have fun making things! True, making things with young children can take time and get a little messy. But it will be fun and it will give them a sense of achievement. Once children start making things, they just might become "crafters" for life.

The Importance of Doing Crafts with Children

The projects that appear in this book were designed for, worked on, and tested by young children and their families. Every craft project in this book highlights at least one task that a young child can perform. Make sure to choose projects with steps that you think your own child can accomplish with relative ease. Remember, what seems like a small, simple task to you—applying glue to the back of a piece of paper, coloring in a simple design, or arranging shells in a dish—is a big accomplishment for a small child, and can instill a sense of pride.

From the time a child picks up his first crayon until he reaches adulthood, he goes through several developmental stages with regard to arts and crafts—from scribbles (about age 2), to assigning meaning to shapes drawn (about age 5); to the creation of three-dimensional objects (about age 8.) Although the pace at which each child progresses may differ, important skills can be developed by working with crafts.

Learning Skills

- Logic, problem solving
- Basic math skills (measuring; using a ruler; using measuring cups)
- Reading (looking at directions or reading a recipe)
- Following sequential directions
- Creativity and artistic sensibility
- Self-esteem and a sense of uniqueness
- Fine and gross motor skills
- Eye-hand coordination
- Cleaning skills (including responsibility)
- Fun!

How to Use This Book

The crafts included here all require the supervision (and usually the hands-on help) of an adult, especially with preschool-aged children. However, each craft contains at least one "kids!" icon (featuring a *Sesame Street* character) indicating a step that your preschooler should be able to accomplish, depending on the skills and abilities of your individual child. Also included with each craft are special features written for the children that bring "words of wisdom" (or just fun thoughts!) from the *Sesame Street* friends.

The first step in creating each craft is to read through the directions for the project from beginning to end. That way you and your child will know what materials and tools you will need. If she is able, encourage her to read familiar numbers out loud from the materials list, and pick out her favorite letters of the alphabet. Although understanding written fractions can be difficult for preschoolers, you can certainly point out "½" in a materials list and explain the concept of "one half" by showing her that if you cut one whole pipe cleaner into two equal parts, you now have two halves.

Finally, although directions for these crafts are often quite specific in order to ensure clarity, remember that part of the fun of making crafts is to be creative. We encourage you to experiment with color, found objects, or decorating in any way that seems appropriate and appealing. Don't worry if the end result doesn't look exactly like the photo. Half the fun of crafting is developing your own style and expression.

A Few Thoughts on Safety

1 **Avoid accidental choking.** It's natural for very young children to put small objects, such as beads, magnets, and crayons, into their mouths. Please supervise your child, no matter what age, at all times. Make it very clear that none of these materials belong in the mouth, then keep a watchful eye.

2 **Keep away from hot or sharp objects.** When making your crafts in the kitchen, be sure you are working at a safe distance from a hot stove and sharp objects, such as knives.

3 **Tie back long hair; roll up sleeves.** Both you and your child should wear an apron, or old clothes, since they might get spattered with glue or paint.

4 **Clean up before and after working with crafts.** Start with a clean work surface so your materials will stay clean. After you've finished, clean up thoroughly.

5 **Work slowly and carefully.** Just do one step at a time.

Get crafty

It's a good idea to keep all your craft materials together. You can design a special craft box, or purchase an inexpensive plastic container from an office supply or container store. Create a special craft "work space" (if you have the space) and cover it with a plastic or paper tablecloth, newspaper or other protection as you work.

Essential Tools

Here's a useful list of essential tools and materials you'll need to do most of the projects in this book.

- Scissors (those with rounded tips are safest for younger children)
- A set of acrylic paints in basic primary colors (red, blue, yellow, black and white)
- Paintbrushes in various sizes and thicknesses
- White glue and an old paintbrush to apply it
- Colored pencils; colored markers; crayons
- Black fine-tipped felt pen
- Pencils
- Ruler
- Large eraser

More useful materials

Here are some other materials you might want to have on hand. Look out for things to collect or interesting materials to store at home until you are ready to craft. This is a great way to reuse things and make less trash in the world.

Gift wrap

Recycled gift wrap can come in handy for many projects. If it's too crumpled, iron it with a cool iron, and it will be as good as new.

Cardboard

Use recycled cardboard from packing boxes, cereal boxes, laundry detergent boxes, or other cardboard packages to make your projects.

Fabric

Worn out blue jeans can be turned into bags, purses, and pencil cases. Scraps of patterned fabric can be used to make bean bags, pouches, as a covering for boxes, or as decorations in infinite ways.

Odds and ends

Save odd buttons, earrings, and other old jewelry in cookie tins, then use them as craft decorations. Even old bottle caps (both metal and plastic) can be used in creative ways.

Objects from nature

When you are outdoors in the park or garden, pick up pretty leaves, interesting twigs, feathers, pine cones, seed heads, stones, and other objects from nature. At the beach collect shells, pebbles, and driftwood.

Tips for success

1 Prepare your space

Cover your workspace with newspaper or a plastic or paper tablecloth. Make sure you and your children are wearing clothes (including shoes!) that you don't mind becoming spattered with food, paint, or glue. But relax! You'll never completely avoid mess; in fact, it's part of the fun!

2 Wash your hands

Wash your hands (and your child's hands) before starting a new project, and clean up as you go along. Clean hands make for clean crafts! Remember to wash hands afterwards too, using soap and warm water to get off any of the remaining materials.

3 Follow steps carefully

Follow each step carefully, and in the sequence in which it appears. We've tested all the projects; we know they work, and we want them to work for you, too. Also, ask your children, if they are old enough, to read along with you as you work through the steps. For a younger child, you can direct her to look at the pictures on the page to try to guess what the next step is.

4 Measure precisely

If a project gives you measurements, use your ruler, T-square, measuring cups, or measuring spoons to make sure you measure as accurately as you can. Sometimes, the success of the project may depend on it. Also, this is a great opportunity to teach measuring techniques to your child.

5 Be patient

You may need to wait while something bakes or leave paint, glue, or clay to dry, sometimes for a few hours or even overnight. Encourage your child to be patient as well; explain to her why she must wait, and, if possible, find ways to entertain her as you are waiting. For example you can show her how long you have to wait by pointing out the time on a clock.

6 Clean up

When you've finished your project, clean up any mess. Store all the materials together so that they are ready for the next time you want to craft. Ask your child to help.

Useful Recipes

Papier-mâché recipe

Papier-mâché is a light, strong molding material made from newspaper (or other paper) and pulped with glue and water. Many different recipes are available, but this one is the easiest.

1 If you want to make a bowl (or any shape), you can cover a balloon with papier-mâché or wrap layers of papier-mâché around a real bowl of the size you wish. If you use a real bowl, smear petroleum jelly over it before you begin to apply the papier-mâché so that the model will slip off easily when it is dry.

You will need
- Newspaper, torn into short strips
- Dish of white glue, mixed with an equal amount of water
- Paintbrush

2 Using a paintbrush, paint the strips of newspaper with the glue mixture. Place the strips one at a time over the object and smooth them down with your hands. Add one layer at a time. Don't put too many layers on at once or the paper will take too long to dry.

Salt dough recipe

Salt dough is an inedible molding material that's easy to make and can be used in many different craft projects.

1 Using your fingers, mix together the flour, salt, and cooking oil in a bowl. Add a little water and mix it in thoroughly until you have a smooth, thick dough, dry enough not to stick to the sides of the bowl. If your mixture is too sticky, simply add more flour; if it's too crumbly, add water.

You will need
- ¾ cup all purpose flour
- 3 tablespoons salt
- 1 teaspoon cooking oil
- ⅓ cup water
- Mixing bowl
- Board

2 Sprinkle a little flour over the board and knead the dough until it is a smooth lump. You can store the dough in a sealed container in the refrigerator for up to three days.

3 Mold your designs. Bake them in a pre-heated oven at 250°F for about 3 hours until firm. Baking times will vary depending on the size and thickness of your object, but make sure it's hard all through.

ELMO'S AWESOME ANIMALS

Fishy glitter globe

This is a great way to use an old jar. Fill it with glittery water, paint on your favorite fish, like Dorothy, and shake up a storm!

You will need

- Empty round jar and lid
- Seashells (optional)
- All-purpose waterproof glue
- Black relief outliner glass paint
- Glass paints: red, orange, green
- Paintbrush
- Water
- Glycerine
- Blue glitter

Kids 1

Arrange shells on the inside of the jar lid. Glue them to the lid and let dry.

2

Turn the jar upside down and, using the black relief paint, draw the outline of fish and seaweed. Let dry.

3

Using the glass paints and brush, color in the seaweed and fish, blending the paints together. Let dry.

4 Fill the jar with water. Add a teaspoon of glitter and a few drops of glycerine.

5 Put a line of glue around the lid and screw it tightly to the top of the jar. Let dry overnight.

Glycerine is great! It makes the water thicker, so when you shake the jar, the glitter falls slowly to the bottom. You can buy it in the home-baking department of your supermarket.

Shake the jar and place it upside down to give your fish a glittery sea to swim in.

Sand butterfly

Elmo is a very busy monster. Elmo is painting a butterfly picture using sand. What will you paint with sand?

You will need

- 8 × 11 inch sheets of cardboard
- 8 × 11 inch sheets of white paper
- Pencil
- Black felt-tip pen
- Scissors
- 11¾ × 16½ inch sheet scrap paper
- White glue and brush
- Colored sand: red, orange, yellow, blue, green
- Teaspoon

1

To make a butterfly, fold the white paper and draw half of its shape on one side. Cut it out. Unfold the shape and put it on the cardboard at an angle.

2

Use the black felt-tip pen to draw around the outline. Add butterfly markings, matching the pattern on each wing.

3

Place the scrap paper under the cardboard. Paste a thin layer of white glue over the butterfly's body and head only.

Scoop some yellow sand into the spoon and sprinkle over the glued area. Lift the picture and gently tap the spare sand onto the scrap paper. Carefully pour the sand back into its container.

Continue gluing and sprinkling until you've finished your picture.

It is I, Grover, your furry adorable globe trotter. I traveled all the way to Italy. Did you know "farfalle" is butterfly-shaped pasta?

Pebble porcupines

Elmo likes making animals from smooth beach pebbles. Elmo is painting pebble porcupines today. What will you paint?

You will need

- 1 large and 2 small smooth stones
- Acrylic paints
- Medium and small paintbrushes
- Clear varnish

1

Wash and dry the stones. Paint them the color of the animal you want to make. Paint an extra coat if you need to. Let dry.

Asking questions is a good way to find out about something you want to know. Like... what is a porcupine? You'll find the answer in step 2.

2

Porcupines are animals with spiky spines or quills. To make pebble porcupines, paint the pebbles gray, let dry, then paint on black bristles.

3

Now add a nose and two eyes, then paint your other pebbles.

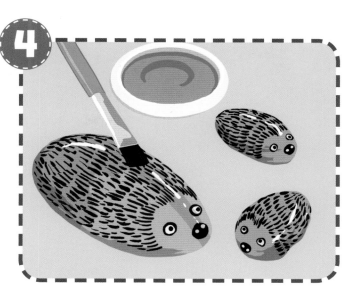

4

If your pebbles are going to live outside on your doorstep or your backyard, give them all a coat of clear varnish.

Elmo has made a scaly fish friend for Dorothy from this long pebble. Elmo is looking in his animal book to see what other creatures he can make from his pebbles.

Animal nests

Nests are warm and safe homes for insects, and reptiles as well as for birds like Rubber Duckie and Big Bird. Make a cozy nest for your toy animals.

You will need

- Medium bag full of thin twigs
- Scissors
- White glue and brush
- Cardboard bowl
- Small brush

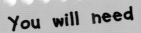

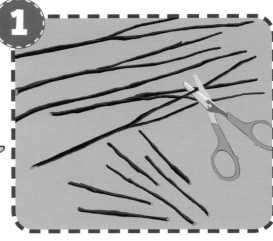

1

Cut the twigs into small pieces about 3-4 inches long.

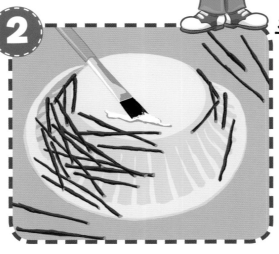

2

Turn the cardboard bowl upside down and brush glue over the outside. Add a layer of twigs over the base and sides of the bowl wherever you spread the glue.

3 kids

Brush glue around the inside of the bowl and add more twigs to the inside, until it looks like a nest.

4

Let dry for about one hour, then fill any gaps with more twigs and let dry.

Rubber Duckie likes nests, but he likes water too. Can you think of any other creatures that like water?

Dinosaur forest

Elmo is using his imagination. He is pretending this "swampy" forest is a mini-world of adventure and discovery.

You will need

- Large plastic pan or tray
- Various vegetable tops (carrots, turnips, parsnips, beets, and pineapples)
- Water
- Toy dinosaurs

1

Cut the tops off some vegetables and fill the plastic plate or tray with a shallow layer of water.

2 kids

Float the vegetable tops on the water with the cut edges down.

3 kids

Set the pan or tray in a warm place. Wait for about 2 weeks for the shoots and leaves to sprout. Make sure to keep water in the pan at all times.

4

After the leaves are tall enough, arrange your toy dinosaurs in the floating forest and make up a fun story about them.

Dinosaurs lived on Earth about 230 million years ago. That's a long time ago!

Birdseed wreath

Elmo wonders if his friend Big Bird will like this natural "birdfeeder." Elmo thinks it looks delicious!

1

With a spoon, spread peanut butter over one side of the bread ring.

You will need

- A loaf of ring-shaped bread
- Peanut butter
- Spoon
- Birdseed
- Shallow dish or plate
- Baking sheet
- Length of ribbon

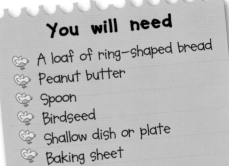

2

Pour birdseed into the dish, then dip the peanut-butter side of the bread ring into the seeds.

3

Bake in the oven for 10 minutes at 425°F.

4

When the bread is cool, tie a ribbon around the top and hang it in your backyard from a nearby tree.

This will be great in winter when it's harder for birds to find food.

Pet photo frame

If you like animals as much as Elmo does, make this cute frame for a picture of your favorite pet or animal.

You will need

- 4 cardboard strips 6 x 1 inch
- 12 Popsicle sticks
- Cardboard (to fit photo)
- 2 different-sized pens (any kind)
- Acrylic paint
- Photo of pet or favorite animal
- Scissors
- Clear adhesive tape

1

Paint the Popsicle sticks and let dry (or use colored ones).

2

Glue 3 Popsicle sticks onto each cardboard strip, leaving about an inch gap at both ends. Then glue the ends of the cardboard strips together into a frame shape.

3

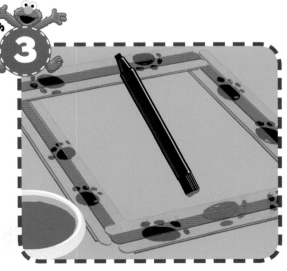

Dip the end of the largest pen into the paint and press down around the frame. Then use the smaller pen to add circles to complete the paw prints.

4

Tape a photo of your pet into the frame then cover the back with a piece of cardboard.

This makes a great gift. I'm going to give mine to my Mommy.

Cress caterpillar

Watercress only takes a few days to grow and it tastes great in salads and sandwiches, too. Elmo loves watercress!

You will need

- 5 egg shells
- Nail scissors
- Paints: green, red, black
- Wobbly eyes
- Paintbrush
- White glue and brush
- Packet of watercress seeds
- Cotton batting
- Red pipe cleaner
- Water

1

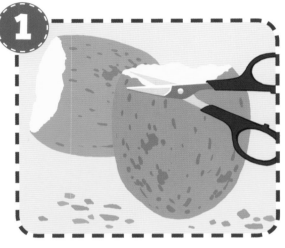

Take 5 clean, empty egg shells with their tops cut off. Trim the top of the egg shells with nail scissors to make them smooth.

2

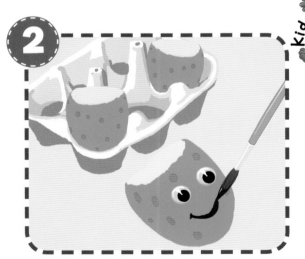

Paint the shells green. Glue wobbly eyes on one shell and paint a mouth. Put all the shells in an egg carton to dry.

kids 3

Once dry, place some cotton batting in the bottom of each shell. Add 1 teaspoon of watercress seeds and a spoonful of water to each shell.

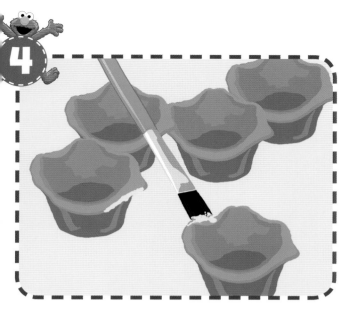

4 Cut up a cardboard egg carton to make five little dishes. Paint them green and glue them together in a wiggly line.

5 Place an egg shell in each dish, with the face at the front. Make antennas by twisting a pipe cleaner into spirals at both ends, fold it in half, then push it into the shell with the face.

Add a little water every other day. Within a week, the watercress will grow. Then you can wash and eat it. I'm going to make a cress salad for my good friend, Snuffy.

Bread dough animals

Elmo loves the smell of fresh baked bread. Uncooked bread is called dough. It's easy to make shapes with bread dough, like these animal shapes.

You will need

- Mixing bowl
- 1 packet active dry yeast
- ⅔ cup warm water
- 1 teaspoon salt
- 1 teaspoon sugar
- ¼ cup unsalted butter
- 1 cup flour
- Raisins

1

In a mixing bowl, dissolve the yeast in the warm water. Stir in the salt and sugar, then add the flour and butter.

2 kids

With your hands, make a ball with the dough and knead it for 5 minutes, or until the dough feels smooth and stretchy.

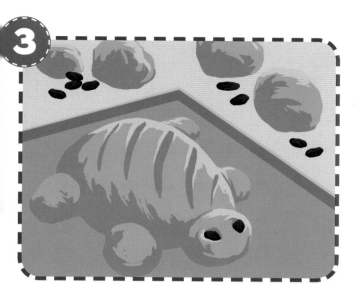

Divide the dough into 3 or 4 smaller pieces and shape into animals, such as a snail, a turtle, a fish, and a snake. Push raisins into the dough for eyes.

Place the animal shapes onto a baking sheet, then leave the dough to rise in a warm place for 30 minutes. Bake in the oven for 20 minutes at 350°F until golden in color. Leave to cool, then enjoy your tasty animal snacks.

Snails and turtles have hard shells. Can you think of any other creatures that have shells?

Animal boots

Elmo can't play outside when it's raining. But when it stops, Elmo keeps his furry feet dry in these fun boots.

You will need

- Old newspaper
- Plain-colored rubber boots
- Felt-tip pen (thin tip)
- Acrylic paint and paintbrush
- Tubed glitter glue
- Wobbly eyes
- White glue and brush

1

Stuff newspaper into the boots so they stay firm. Using the felt-tip pen, draw some shapes on them.

2

Paint the bigger areas with paint. Let dry. Add another coat of paint if necessary.

3

Carefully squeeze out the glitter glue into whatever shapes you like. Add more paint, if necessary.

4

Glue the wobbly eyes onto the boots. Let dry in a warm, dry place.

For me, I love yucchy rainy days. What's your favorite kind of weather?

33

Glove painting

This is so much fun! Elmo loves to paint animals and other creatures while wearing gloves! Why don't you give it a try too?

You will need

- Acrylic paints: pink, blue, orange, yellow and green
- Shallow container (to put paint into)
- Latex gloves or kids' gardening gloves
- White paper
- Paintbrush
- Wobbly eyes (optional)
- White glue and brush

1

Pour a small amount of paint into the shallow container.

kids 2

To make bugs: Using a different finger for each color, dip into the paint and print the color onto paper. Let dry.

kids 3

To make an owl: Using a big brush, paint onto the side of your hand and print onto another sheet of paper. Let dry.

4

Add arms, legs, and faces to your paintings and prints to turn them into creatures. Add wobbly eyes, if you wish.

Why not try making some bugs from your fingerprints?

Remember to wash your gloves so you can use them again next time you want to make a glove picture.

35

Seaside flower pot

Elmo likes to reuse things. When Elmo has eaten some yummy yogurt, he washes the container and turns it into a vase for some flowers!

1 kids

Paint the pot white to cover any printing, then let dry. When the paint is dry, use a pencil to draw an underwater scene onto the container.

2 kids

Color in the scene with paints and let dry. Arrange some pretty flowers in the pot.

These flowers smell so pretty. I have a long trunk to smell them. What do you use to smell things?

ZOES'S FUN WITH PAPER

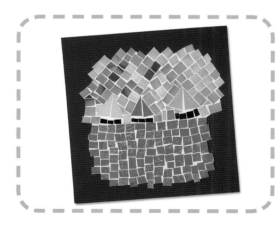

Ballerina card

I love everything about ballet. I'm going to make a special ballerina card to give to my friend. Can you help me?

You will need

- White cardboard 8 inches square
- Pencil
- Set of colored pencils
- Blue paper 6 x 12 inches
- Scissors
- White glue and brush

1

Fold the card in half. In the middle, draw a ballet dancer. Don't draw her tutu just yet...you'll find out why in step 3.

2

Color in the ballerina using your favorite colored pencils. Try to stay inside the lines when you're coloring in.

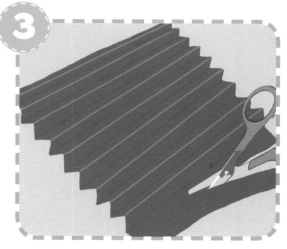

3

For the ballerina's tutu, make folds along the shorter side of the blue paper, about ½ inch apart. Trim off any extra folds at the end of the paper.

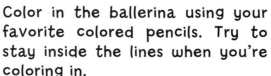

4 Fold the paper in half so that the two shorter edges are together. Cut a small piece of blue paper, fold it in half, and glue it where the two ends meet, making a fan shape.

5 Glue along the edge of the fan. Put the fold in the middle of the card at the ballerina's waist and stick the 2 edges down. Fold the card closed.

Now open your card. Ta da! The ballerina's tutu has popped out. Give your card to a friend.

Bubble gift wrap

Now I'm making some bubbly gift wrap with Prairie Dawn. It's so much fun! Why don't you give it a try?

You will need

- Old newspapers
- Acrylic paints: red, blue
- Dishwashing liquid
- Water
- Old spoon
- Drinking straws
- Shallow bowl
- White paper
- Measuring spoons

1

Cover your work surface with newspaper. Using a spoon, stir together ½ cup water, 1 or 2 tablespoons red paint, and ½ tablespoon dishwashing liquid in the bowl.

2 kids

Place a straw in the paint mixture and gently blow to make bubbles. Keep blowing until the bubbles are almost at the edge of the dish.

3 Put a piece of paper on top of the bubbles and hold it there until several bubbles have popped. Move the paper and continue popping bubbles until most of the paper has been colored. Don't push the paper too far into the bowl.

4 Clean the bowl and make a blue paint mixture. Repeat steps 1 to 3 so you have a blue and red bubbly pattern on the piece of paper. Let dry before using the paper.

Add a drop more dishwashing liquid to make more bubbles. If the bubbles are too faint on the paper, add more paint to the mixture.

Printed star card

Rosita is helping me make this card out of paint, foam, and some thick cardboard. Do you want to have a go?

You will need

- Sheet of blue cardboard 6 × 12 inches, folded in half
- Tracing paper and pencil
- Scissors
- 3 pieces foam 2 × 2 inches
- 3 pieces thick cardboard 2 × 2 inches
- Acrylic paints: red, yellow, dark blue and a brush
- White glue and brush
- Red glitter

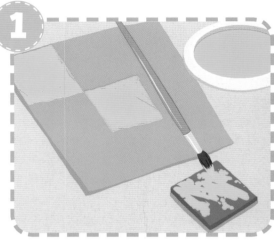

Glue a foam square onto a square of thick cardboard to create a stamp. Add yellow paint and print 5 squares in the corners and middle of the blue card. Let dry.

Draw a star onto the tracing paper. Trace the shape onto the foam to make 2 stars. Cut out.

Stick each star to a square of thick cardboard. Add blue paint to one of the star stamps and print a star onto each blue square.

Use the other star stamp to print red stars on the yellow squares. Let dry.

Mix a little water with glue and brush it onto the middle, top left, and bottom right red stars. Sprinkle red glitter over the glued stars and shake off any excess glitter. Let dry.

Greeting cards are given to celebrate a special time with someone. In Mexico, the country where I was born, we speak Spanish. "Feliz Cumpleaños" means Happy Birthday!

Paper airplanes

Elmo is my best friend. He is making paper planes with Ernie and Super Grover. Oh boy! I'd better watch out!

1

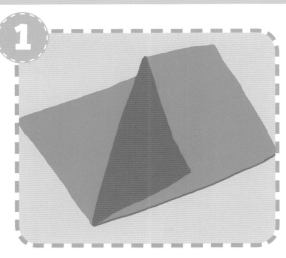

Fold the sheet of paper in half. Turn down the corners at one end so that the folded-down edges line up along your fold.

2

To make the wings, fold the top down again, lining it up along the bottom of the shape. Repeat on the other side.

3

Fold the top flaps down again, lining them up along the bottom of the airplane.

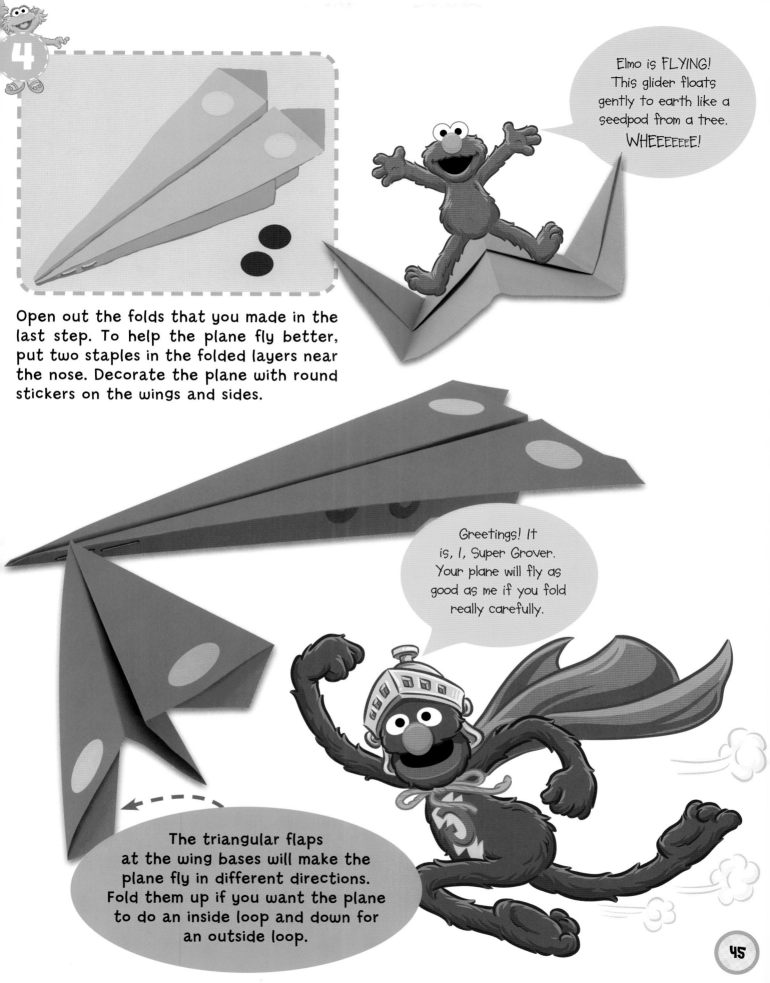

4

Open out the folds that you made in the last step. To help the plane fly better, put two staples in the folded layers near the nose. Decorate the plane with round stickers on the wings and sides.

Elmo is FLYING! This glider floats gently to earth like a seedpod from a tree. WHEEEEEEE!

Greetings! It is, I, Super Grover. Your plane will fly as good as me if you fold really carefully.

The triangular flaps at the wing bases will make the plane fly in different directions. Fold them up if you want the plane to do an inside loop and down for an outside loop.

45

Gift wrap

We've used club, spade, heart, and diamond shapes for the gift wrap pattern but you can choose other shapes.

You will need

- 4 scraps thin cardboard, 2¼ inch square
- Pencil
- Scissors
- Tissue paper
- Gold paint
- Saucer
- Piece of sponge (e.g. dishwashing sponge)
- Hole punch
- Thin gold ribbon

1

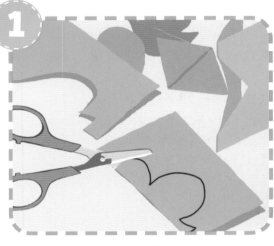

Fold each piece of cardboard in half. Draw half of any shape you like against each fold. Cut out the shapes.

kids 2

Place the cardboard with the spade-shaped hole onto the paper. Dab the sponge in the paint then dab the paint over the hole. Remove the card when the paint is dry.

kids 3

Do the same with the other 3 shapes and continue printing all over the paper.

4

Make gift tags out of the cut-out shapes you set aside in step 1. Simply punch a hole in them and thread a piece of thin ribbon through the hole.

Hey everybody! What's all the excitement? Do you like the gift wrap? Try using circles, triangles, squares, and rectangles. It's a swell idea.

Tissue paper card

Baby Bear is showing me how to make a card for my best friend, Elmo. Why don't you give it a try too!

1

Make sure your hands are clean. Then fold the white cardboard in half.

You will need

- 8½ × 11 inch sheet of white cardboard
- 3 sheets of tissue paper in different colors
- Pencil
- Scissors
- White glue mixed with equal amount of water and brush

2

Fold a sheet of tissue paper in half. Lightly draw one half of your favorite shape next to the fold. (When you tear or cut it out and unfold it, you'll have a whole shape!) We chose a heart shape.

3

Carefully tear or cut the shape out of the tissue paper. Make more shapes on the other sheets of tissue.

4

Carefully brush the glue onto the shapes and stick them onto the card. Make the shapes overlap each other.

5

Make a frame for your design. For example, roughly tear thin strips from the leftover tissue and stick them around the edges of the card to make a border.

I'm going to give this card to my mommy. Who are you going to give your card to?

Paper pom-poms

Make your presents look really special with paper pom-pom decorations. Go pom-pom crazy with me!

You will need

- 2 sheets of tissue paper in different shades of the same color
- Scissors
- White glue and brush

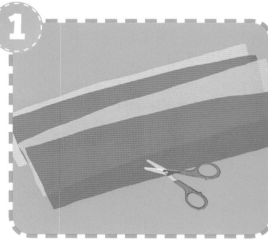

1

Cut out 2 strips about an inch wide from each sheet of colored tissue paper.

2

Brush glue along the bottom edge of each strip and glue all 4 strips together.

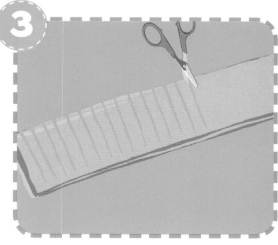

3

Use scissors to snip along the strips, making each cut about ½ inch apart. Don't cut all the way through.

Spread glue along the bottom of the strip and roll the shape up. Press it together at the bottom and let dry.

Use your fingers to fluff out the pom-pom. Dab some glue on the bottom and stick on top of a present.

I'm going to make my pom-pom from recycled paper. Or you can make a pom-pom using shimmery foil paper and pinking shears for a spiky look.

Designer envelopes

Here's a special envelope for a homemade card. Why don't you make one too?

You will need

- Sheet of 8½ × 11 inch colored paper
- Scissors
- Patterned gift wrap
- Gluestick
- Homemade card

1

Put your handmade card on the sheet of colored paper. Fold the paper in on two sides and the bottom. Then fold over the top of the paper to make the flap.

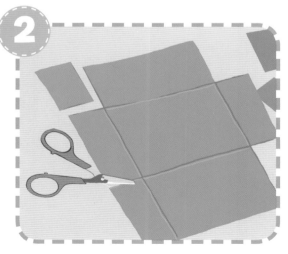

2

Unfold the paper and cut out the four small corner rectangles.

3

Cut a piece of gift wrap to fit in the top flap and main area. Leave ½ inch gap around the edge of the gift wrap. Glue in place. Trim the corners of the top and side flaps.

Fold up the bottom flap, then fold in the sides and glue them in place. Place the homemade card inside, then fold down and glue the top flap.

You can make a colorful envelope from patterned paper. Don't forget to add a label with the name of the person you're giving the card to on the front.

You can also add colorful stickers to decorate your envelope.

Bert

Mosaic boat scene

Mosaic is the art of creating pictures from small pieces of glass, stone or other material. We are making a mosaic picture using scraps of paper.

You will need

- Old magazines
- Scissors
- 8½ x 11 inch sheet of white paper and pencil
- White glue and brush
- Large sheet of colored paper

kids 1

Choose colored sections of old magazines to make your picture. We're making a boat scene, so we need blues and greens.

2

Cut the scraps into squares of roughly the same size, about ½ inch.

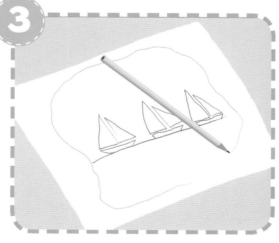

3

Lightly draw your scene on the white paper. Draw a line around your picture to create a frame.

4

Start placing the squares onto your picture. When you are happy with the look, glue the squares down.

5

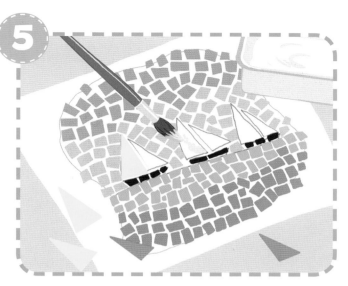

We're making triangle shapes for the boat sails. Finish off by cutting around the picture and gluing it to colored paper.

I love triangle shapes. What's your favorite shape?

Wastepaper basket

Wastepaper baskets and garbage cans can be beautiful. Cover yours in some brightly colored gift wrap.

You will need

- Round cardboard waste basket
- Roll of gift wrap
- Scissors
- White glue diluted with equal amount of water
- Paintbrush

kids

1

Choose gift wrap that you like. Cut a piece a bit larger than the container. Wrap the paper around the container and glue it in place.

2

Make small snips in the top and bottom edges, fold them over and glue them down.

Ask a grown up about recycling the paper once you've filled your basket.

OSCAR'S TOP TRASH CRAFTS

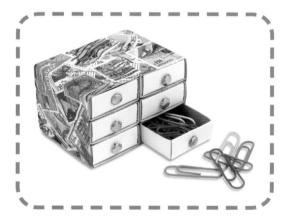

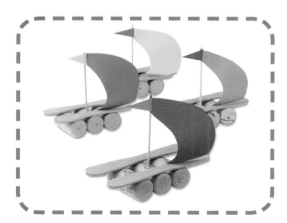

Bird feeder

Recycling is a good way to use old things in a new way. For example, turn an old juice carton into a bird feeder.

You will need

- Empty, rinsed-out juice carton with a nozzle
- Sandpaper
- Scissors
- Acrylic paints
- Paintbrush
- Bird seed
- Garden wire
- Mesh netting bag
- Varnish

1

Rub the outside of the carton with sandpaper until it's rough. Cut out a rectangular hole on the side facing away from the nozzle.

Kids

2

Paint the carton all over in one color. This one is brown to look like tree bark.

Kids

3

After the paint is dry, add different shades and colors. This one has knots and vines, just like bark.

4

Add leaves or other decorations in a different color. When you've finished painting, add a coat of varnish to help protect the feeder during cold and wet months.

5

Fill the mesh netting bag with birdseed, then push it through the rectangular hole in the feeder. Remove the nozzle, then pull the top of the bag through the spout. Next, thread wire through the top of the bag and twist the ends together. Hang the feeder up outside.

That's so magic—the old juice carton is now a bird feeder!

Indoor garden

Make a plant pot for herbs, bulbs or seeds. This is my kind of mess.

You will need

- 3 yogurt containers
- Sandpaper
- Acrylic paints
- 3 carton lids
- Potted herbs, bulbs or seeds
- Soil mix
- Awl or screwdriver

1 Wash and dry the containers and gently rub all over the outsides with sandpaper. This will help the paint to stick to the pots.

2 Make holes in the bottom of each pot with an awl or screwdriver.

Brush two coats of paint on the outside of each pot. When the paint has dried, add a pattern, like these white dots, on each pot.

Paint some carton lids in bright colors to make matching saucers.

5

Remove the herbs, bulbs or seeds from their pots and repot them. Add extra soil to fill the pots. Press it down and water well.

Elmo added wobbly eyes and a smiley mouth to his plant pot. What other designs can you put on yours?

Designer shoes

Use a clean pair of canvas shoes or sneakers for this craft, and personalize them with your own pictures and patterns.

kids 1

Use the paint to draw and color pictures on your sneakers. Here are scary skulls. Boo! Let dry.

You will need

- Pair of clean sneakers or canvas shoes
- Fabric paints
- Fabric pens
- Glitter
- Plastic gemstones
- Beads

kids 2

Next, add some more detail in a different colored paint, like these flames. Let dry.

3

Once you've finished your design on both shoes, leave them to dry thoroughly.

Sometimes the paint shrinks a little as it dries and flakes off. Touch up with some fresh paint if needed.

Now you're ready to wear your totally unique footwear.

I've given my ballet slippers a pretty princess look, by gluing glitter and plastic gemstones onto the shoes, then drawing patterns with the fabric pens. Finally, I threaded beads onto the laces.

Chest of drawers

Bert has created this chest to tidy up a lot of little things, from paper clips to stamps. Me? I prefer messes.

You will need

- 6 empty matchboxes
- White glue and brush
- Selection of old/used stamps
- Scissors
- 6 brass paper fasteners

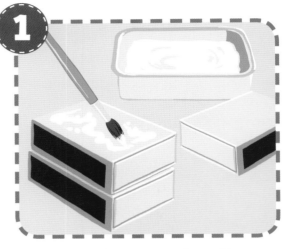

1 Glue 3 matchboxes together on top of one another. Do the same with the remaining 3 matchboxes.

2 Glue the 2 sets of matchboxes together side by side. Let dry.

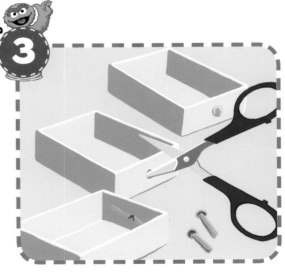

3 Remove the drawers. Use the end of a small pair of scissors to make a hole in the middle of each drawer. Push a paper fastener into each hole and bend the ends to fix them in place.

4

Paint the backs of the stamps with glue and stick them on the matchboxes. Overlap the stamps and stick them on at different angles to make a fun design.

5

Trim the stamps where they overlap the edges of the box. Put the drawers back inside the boxes.

I love spending time with my paperclip collection. What will you keep in your chest of drawers?

Striped coin saver

The Count has made this striped coin saver. Use an empty potato chip can. Start saving your spare money and you'll be filthy rich before you know it!

You will need

- Empty cardboard container with lid
- Ruler and pencil
- Several 8½ × 11 inch sheets of colored paper
- White glue and brush
- Craft knife or box cutter

1 Measure the height of the container and cut the paper to the same height. Draw narrow and wide lines down one sheet.

2 Put the ruled sheet with the lines drawn on it on top of the others and cut along the lines to make long strips.

3 Paint the strips with glue and stick them to the can, making sure they overlap and smoothing them down carefully.

4

After the glue has dried, cut a slot measuring about 2 x ¼ inches.

Purple is my favorite color. What's yours? Do you mind if I count the coins while you decide?

Tiger paws

Turn old tissue boxes into wild feet, like these tiger paws—maybe even your favorite monster's feet from Sesame Street.

You will need

- 2 empty tissue boxes
- Acrylic paints
- Paintbrush and old sponge
- Black funky foam
- 10 double-sided adhesive tabs or tape
- Scissors
- White glue and brush

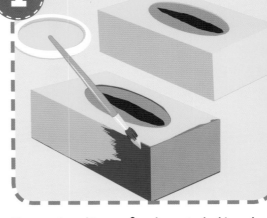

1

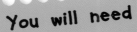

To make tiger feet paint the top and sides of the tissue boxes yellow, then let dry.

2

Dip a dry sponge in orange paint and dab it all over the boxes. Let dry.

3

Paint black stripes all over the boxes. Let dry.

4

Cut out claws from the black foam. Glue them onto the box using double-sided adhesive tabs on top.

Hey everybody. My feet are large and furry. What kind of feet will you make?

Racing sailboats

Rub-a-dub! I don't like getting clean but these little boats make washing in the tub more fun.

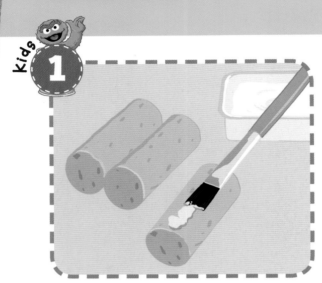

1

Glue the corks together, side by side. Let dry.

You will need

For each boat:
- 3 corks
- White glue and brush
- 2 Popsicle sticks
- Toothpick
- Scraps of colored paper

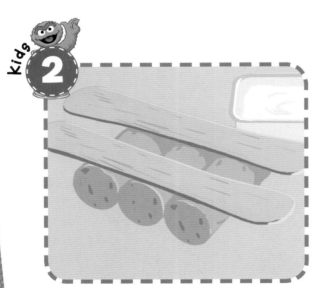

2

Glue the two Popsicle sticks to the top of the corks as shown. Let dry.

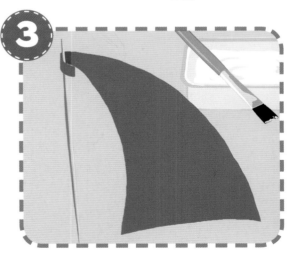

3

Cut a triangular sail from some colored paper. Apply a little glue to the tip of the sail and wrap it around the top of the toothpick mast. Let dry.

4

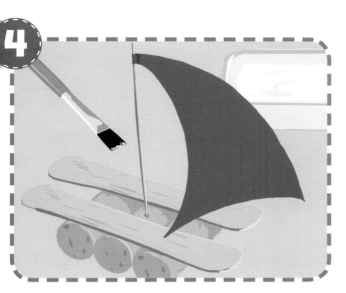

Make a hole in the center of the middle cork between the sticks. Push the toothpick mast into the hole. Bend the sail so it sits on the top of the boat.

5

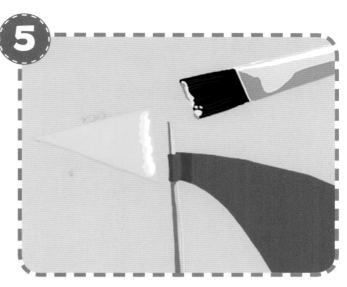

Cut a tiny triangle in yellow paper and glue to the top of the toothpick mast to make a flag.

Rubber Duckie floats in the water, just like these little boats do. Can you name something else that floats in water?

Sporty storage box

Even better than my trash can, this box is perfect for storing sports equipment. Or you could make a box for toys, art materials, or just your favorite things.

You will need

- Large cardboard box with lid
- Large and small paintbrushes
- Acrylic paints
- Pencil
- Paper
- Scissors
- White glue and brush

kids

Paint the box and the lid in your favorite color. Leave to dry, then paint a second coat.

Draw different pieces of sport equipment (or whatever designs you wish) onto the white paper. Cut them out.

Use paints to color in the sporting shapes.

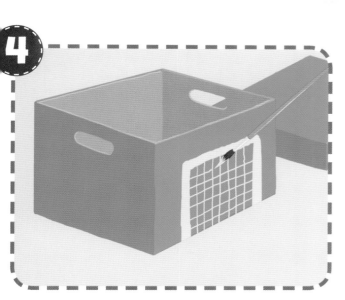

If you wish, paint a large white soccer net, or some other design onto the front of the box.

Arrange all the sports shapes around the box and glue them on.

Go Team Elmo! Elmo loves playing sports with his friends. Which sport is Elmo playing today?

Starry pen tube

Make a tube to hold pens, pencils, or crayons for yourself or give it as a gift. This one is designed like the night sky with stars and comets.

1

Lightly rub the tube all over with sandpaper. This will help the paint stick better to the tube.

You will need

- Cardboard tube with lid
- Fine sandpaper
- Black acrylic paint
- Paintbrush
- White glue and brush
- Glitter: gold, silver
- Scrap paper
- Sequins and star stickers

Kids 2

Cover the tube in black acrylic paint. Let dry, then apply another coat. Let the can dry thoroughly.

Kids 3

Brush some glue onto the tube then sprinkle the glitter over the top. Shake off the excess glitter onto a piece of scrap paper.

4

Add the star stickers. Glue a row of sequins around the top and bottom of the tube, or anywhere to make your pen tube shimmer.

Stars shine brightly at night. I love to look up at the stars. They're so beautiful!

Popsicle stick pot

Keep all your colored pencils or crayons in this pot, or even put a little plant in it. You can decorate it with paints or stickers if you like.

You will need

- Empty cardboard tube
- About 30 Popsicle sticks of the same size
- Small set square (triangle)
- White glue and brush

1

Wash the Popsicle sticks and tube. When dry, line up the set square against the tube and glue the Popsicle stick in place, aligning it with the set square. Let dry.

2

Glue the sticks around the tube, until it's completely covered. Make sure the Popsicle sticks align snugly.

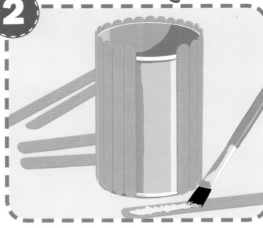

COOKIE MONSTER'S FUN FOOD

Choc chunk cookies

Me hear you say the word "cookie." Can me make these delicious cookies with you?

You will need

- Large mixing bowl
- Sieve
- 2¼ cups all-purpose flour
- Pinch of salt
- 1 teaspoon baking powder
- 1 tablespoon butter
- ¾ cup light brown sugar
- 2 eggs, beaten
- 2 ounces corn syrup
- 3 ounces semi-sweet chocolate
- Rolling pin
- A cookie cutter
- Nonstick cooking spray
- Baking sheet

1

Pre-heat the oven to 325°F. Sift the flour, salt, and baking powder into a large bowl.

kids 2

With your fingers, rub the butter into the dry ingredients. Add the sugar. In a cup, stir together the eggs and the corn syrup.

kids 3

With a wooden spoon, beat the ingredients until they are thoroughly combined. Break the chocolate into small chunks and add to the mixture.

Place the dough on a board. Sprinkle it lightly with flour so it doesn't stick to the rolling pin. Roll out the dough until it's about ½-inch thick. With a cookie cutter, cut out the cookies, like these star-shaped cookies.

Lightly grease a baking sheet with nonstick cooking spray or vegetable oil. Place the cookies about 2 inches apart on the baking sheet. Bake for about 15 minutes, until golden.

Fruit smoothies

Me love smoothies almost as much as cookies! M-M-M-M-M!

You will need

For a strawberry and mango smoothie:

- 4 strawberries
- ¾ cup sliced mango
- 1 small banana
- Juice of 1 orange
- 3 tablespoons low fat yogurt
- 1 tablespoon honey
- Blender container
- Glass and straws

1

Chop three strawberries, the mango, and the banana. Put them in the bowl of the blender with all the other ingredients.

2

Blend everything until you have a smooth, thick mixture.

3

Pour the smoothie into a glass. Cut the remaining strawberry in half and use it to decorate the glass. Add straws.

Elmo loves smoothies. You can make them with pineapple, blueberries, peaches, or lots of other fruit you like!

It is very hot in Mexico so we eat Popsicles to keep cool. Why not make a fruit Popsicle using your smoothie? Just pour the mixture into a tray, add a Popsicle stick, and put it in the freezer!

Pasta jewelry

Now me making pasta jewelry with Zoe. You can use these shapes and colors, or choose your own.

1 kids

Paint the pasta wheels in green, blue, and purple acrylic paint, or any colors you like.

You will need

- Dried pasta shapes: 6 wheels, 24 curly macaroni
- Acrylic paints: green, blue, purple, gold
- Lump of modeling clay
- Toothpicks
- Colored string, elastic, or cord

2 kids

Paint the macaroni gold, and put all the shapes on the ends of toothpicks stuck into a large piece of modeling clay.

Tie a button to the string while you thread the shapes to keep them from falling off!

3

Thread three macaronis then a wheel onto the colored string or cord. Repeat this until all the pasta is threaded.

4

Knot the two ends of the string together, making sure you have made your necklace big enough to go over your head.

There are a lot of different pasta shapes, like wheels or bowties. Which one is your favorite?

Gingerbread men

This no cookie. Me and Ernie making gingerbread cookie to eat. Ya-ya.

You will need

To make 10 gingerbread men:
- 2 tablespoons butter
- ½ cup brown sugar
- ¼ cup (4 tablespoons) molasses
- 1 cup plus 2 tablespoons all-purpose flour
- Pinch of salt
- ½ teaspoon each: baking powder, ginger, cinnamon
- Gingerbread man cutter
- Rolling pin, baking sheet, sieve, bowl, saucepan
- Frosting: ½ cup confectioner's sugar, water, blue food coloring, plastic sandwich bag

1

Heat the butter, molasses, and sugar gently in a pan until the sugar dissolves and the butter melts.

2

Sift together the flour, salt, baking powder, ginger, and cinnamon into a large bowl. Add the sugar mixture, and with a wooden spoon, mix well.

3

Form the dough into a ball, wrap it in plastic wrap, and refrigerate for at least an hour. Then, roll the dough out to about ½-inch thick.

4

Pre-heat oven to 350°F. Grease a baking sheet. Using the cutter, cut out the cookies. Place them 2-inches apart on a baking sheet; bake for 8-12 minutes, depending upon size of the cookies. Let cool.

5

To make the frosting: sift the confectioner's sugar into a bowl, add a few drops of food coloring, and a little water. Mix until the frosting is thick but still a bit runny.

6

Make a pastry bag by snipping the corner off a plastic sandwich bag, then spooning the frosting into the top. Gently squeeze the frosting onto the cookies.

You can make gingerbread boys by using a smaller cookie cutter. Make gingerbread ladies and girls, too!

Treasure map

Me hope this map leads to a cookie treasure. Me need cookie treat after a big adventure!

You will need

- Sheet of thick construction paper
- Bowl of warm water
- Instant coffee granules
- Paper towels
- Felt-tip pens

kids 1

Tear the edges from all around the sheet of paper to give it rough edges.

kids 2

Crumple the sheet of paper up into a ball so that it is really creased.

kids 3

Flatten the paper and dip it into a bowl of warm water. Put the wet paper on a draining board and sprinkle a spoonful of coffee granules over the paper.

4

Dab the stains with paper towels to soak up any extra moisture, then dip the paper in a bowl of warm water. Repeat the staining and rinsing on the other side of the paper. Let dry.

5

Draw a treasure map like the one shown. Identify dangerous areas with a skull and crossbones and mark the hidden treasure with a big "X."

Shhh! Elmo is being very quiet. Elmo wants to find the treasure on this map. Can you see the big red "X"? Oh very good. Elmo can see it now too...

Fishy burgers

Me LOVE cookies but me like fishy burgers, too. Do you like burgers or cookies or BOTH?

You will need

To make 4 burgers:

- Vegetable oil
- 1 small onion, chopped
- 1 teaspoon chopped parsley (or herb of choice)
- ½ cup breadcrumbs
- 8-ounce can red salmon or tuna packed with water
- 1 egg
- Salt and pepper to taste
- Flour
- Lettuce, tomato slices, onion rings, mayonnaise
- 4 wholewheat burger buns
- Skillet

kids 1

Heat 2 teaspoonfuls of oil in the skillet; add the onion, herbs, and breadcrumbs and saute gently for 5 minutes.

kids 2

Pour the mixture into a bowl and let cool. Add the fish, egg, salt, and pepper. Mix everything together with your hands.

kids 3

Sprinkle some flour onto the work surface and shape the mixture into burgers.

Wash and dry the skillet, add oil, and place over medium heat. Fry the burger for 5 minutes on each side.

Put each burger on a bun and garnish with lettuce, tomato slices, onion rings, and mayonnaise.

It says here that you can use tuna instead of salmon. The smellier, the better, I say!

Veggie print shirt

Me don't just eat food. Me can use food for other things, such as making a hand-printed T-shirt like this one.

You will need

- Clean white T-shirt
- Piece of scrap cardboard
- Vegetables: 1 large potato, 1 small potato, 1 stalk of celery, 1 carrot
- Cutting board and knife
- Fabric paint (green or color of choice)
- Shallow dish
- Tube of fabric relief paint (metallic blue or color of choice)

1

Cut the two potatoes in half and trim the top of the celery. Cut a 1¼ inch piece of carrot; then cut it in half lengthways.

kids

2

Place cardboard inside the shirt to stop the paint from seeping through. To make the frog's body: dip a large potato half into the paint, and print it in the center of the T-shirt.

kids

3

Use one of the small potato halves to print the two back legs. Dip the top end of the celery stalk into the paint and use to print his bulging eyes.

4

Use the carrot to print the lower back legs and the front legs, then cut the carrot piece in half to print the front and back feet. Let dry.

5

Dab tiny spots all over the frog, using the tube of fabric paint. Let the T-shirt dry thoroughly.

This cute gecko was also made with potato, carrot, and celery, with yellow relief paint dotted over its body. Can you think of any other animal shapes you can make with vegetables?

Tasty cupcakes

A cupcake is almost as good as cookie. Me have fun making them and me have even more fun eating them.

1

Mix the butter and sugar in a large bowl. Mix in the egg a little at a time. Add a few drops of vanilla extract.

You will need

To make 12 cakes:
- ¼ cup butter
- Heaped ¼ cup sugar
- 1 egg, beaten
- Vanilla extract
- ¾ cup self-rising flour
- Foil mini bake cups
- Wooden spoon, dessert spoon, cookie sheet, sieve, and cooling rack

- For the frosting:
- ½ cup confectioner's sugar
- Few drops red food coloring
- Metallic cake decorations
- Butter knife and butter

kids 2

Sift the flour into the bowl. Using a wooden spoon, mix it in gently to make a batter.

kids 3

Pre-heat the oven to 400°F. Place 2 tablespoons of batter into each cup. Put them on a cookie sheet and bake for 10 minutes. Let them cool.

4

To make the frosting, sift the confectioner's sugar into a bowl. Add a few drops of food coloring and just enough water to make a paste.

kids 5

Spread the frosting onto the cakes. Sprinkle metallic balls or other decorations on top and let the frosting set.

The word "cupcake" starts with the letter C. Think of some other foods that start with the letter C.

Peppermint candies

Me needs help making these scrumptious sweets, but me needs no help eating them!

You will need

To make 20 candies:
- 4 cups confectioner's sugar
- 1 egg white
- Juice of half a lemon
- A few drops of peppermint extract
- Green food coloring
- Bar of semi-sweet chocolate
- Sieve, bowl, cookie cutter, wooden spoon, saucepan

1 kids

Sift the confectioner's sugar into a large mixing bowl.

2

Separate the egg yolk from the white. Add the egg white to the confectioner's sugar.

3 kids

With your hands or a spoon, mix it together until you have made a soft lump. Add the lemon juice, peppermint extract, and food coloring.

Pour the lump onto a cold surface and flatten it to about ½ inch thick. With a cookie cutter, cut out the shapes, put them on a baking sheet, and leave them in a cool, dry place to set for around 30 minutes.

Break up the bar of chocolate and put it in a bowl. Put the bowl over a saucepan of simmering water and stir the chocolate until it has melted.

6

Take the bowl off the heat and quickly dip half of each candy into the chocolate. Leave the candies until the chocolate hardens.

You could make fruit chocs instead. Dip strawberries, cherries, and sliced apple in the melted chocolate. Phew! All this dipping can make a monster dizzy.

Banana sundae

Me tummy full. But me want to try this banana sundae. The other fruit sundaes look yummy, too!

You will need
- Vanilla ice cream
- 1 banana
- Chocolate sauce
- Candy sprinkles
- Sundae glass and spoon

1

Spoon ice cream into the bottom of a sundae dish.

2

Add a layer of sliced banana and some chocolate sauce. Then add more ice cream. Repeat the layers until you have only 3 slices of banana left.

3

Decorate the top of the sundae with the banana slices, some additional chocolate sauce, and the sprinkles.

Fresh strawberries and raspberry ripple ice cream make a tasty fruity sundae.

This delicious sundae is made with peach ice cream, peach slices, and crushed meringue.

97

Clove pomanders

Clove pomanders make everything smell delicious! Very spicy, like a spice cookie!

You will need

- 1 orange and 1 lime
- ½ yard green ribbon; ½ yard red ribbon
- Toothpick
- Cloves

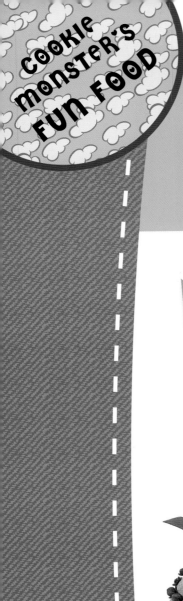

Look! The bows are the same shape as my barrettes!

kids 1

Put the orange in the middle of the green ribbon. Tie the ribbon in a knot then tie a tight bow over the knot. Repeat for the lime, using the red ribbon.

kids 2

Use a toothpick to pierce the orange, then push a clove into the hole. Make holes all over the orange, about ¼ inch apart. Insert one clove in each hole. Repeat for the lime.

PRAIRIE DAWN'S GREAT GIFTS

Foil frame

Make a perfect picture frame from foil and old cardboard. Nobody will ever guess you've been recycling!

You will need

- Thick cardboard 5 × 5 inches
- Thin cardboard 6 × 6 inches
- Ruler
- Scissors
- Tin foil 8 × 8 inches
- White glue and brush
- Old ballpoint pen
- Small photo

1 Measure and cut out a 2 x 2 inch square hole from the middle of the thick cardboard.

2 Glue the card to the non-shiny side of the foil. Make a hole in the foil and make cuts toward each corner. Fold the triangles you've made onto the back of the frame and glue them down.

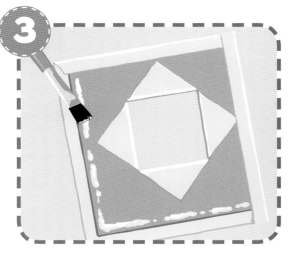

3 Put a line of glue round the cardboard and glue the 4 foil edges to it.

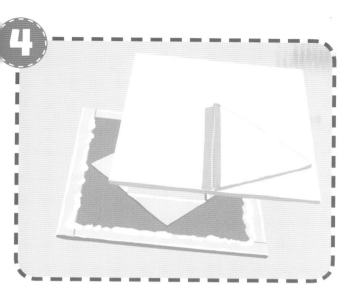

To make a stand, cut out a triangle of cardboard and tape it to the square of thin card as shown. Then glue the two squares of card together around three sides, leaving a slot at the top.

Slide a photo into the slot in the frame. Using the empty ballpoint pen, mark your design on the frame. Don't press too hard or you may tear the foil.

You could even cut out a heart-shaped frame and decorate it with heart shapes cut from foil candy wrappers.

Felt beads

My grandmother showed me how to make these necklaces. Just roll up and glue colored squares of felt, then cut slices to make spiral-patterned beads.

You will need

- Felt squares 3 x 3 inches: yellow, pink, and black
- White glue and brush
- Scissors
- 2 rubber bands
- Needle and gold thread
- 18 small black beads

1 Spread glue thinly onto the black square and stick the pink square on top. Now spread glue onto the pink square and stick the yellow square to it.

2 Spread glue thinly onto the yellow square and roll up the layers to make a Swiss-roll shape.

3 Hold the roll in place with a rubber band at each end and let dry.

4

Remove the rubber bands and cut the roll into slices about ½ inch wide. Choose the best beads for your necklace.

5

Tie a knot in the thread about 4 inches from the end. Thread on three black beads, then push the needle through the top of one of the felt beads near the join. Thread three more black beads, then the next felt bead. Continue until you have used all the beads. Tie a knot in the thread and trim the end.

Make a pendant by gluing three felt beads together. Thread the beads on as shown. Push the needle through the top of your trio of beads.

Candy cushions

These comfy, candy-shaped cushions look good enough to eat. Make a pile and turn your bedroom into a candy store!

kids 1

Glue the two pieces of fabric together, one on top of the other, along the longer edges. Glue the short edges together to make a tube. Put newspaper inside to stop the glued seam from sticking to the other side.

You will need

For each cushion:
- 1 piece of gold-colored fabric 20 x 28 inches
- 1 piece of colored netting 20 x 28 inches
- Newspaper
- White glue and brush
- 2 strong rubber bands
- Cushion filling, such as polyester filling
- ½ yard gold ribbon

2

Once dry, gather up one end about 5 inches from the edge and hold it in place with one of the rubber bands.

kids 3

Start stuffing the cushion with the filling until it is filled to about 5 inches from the top.

4

Close the end with the other rubber band. Fan out the ends of the cushion to make them look like candy wrappers.

5

Glue some gold ribbon over the rubber bands so they don't show.

Recycle old cushions by picking apart the seams and reusing the filling for your groovy new cushions. It's so enchanting!

Friendship bracelet

Show your best friend how much you like them with this great friendship bracelet.

You will need

- 🍓 4 strands of cotton thread: 2 mauve, 1 pink and 1 purple (or the colors of your choice), each 20 inches long
- 🍓 1 large bead and 4 medium-sized beads

kids

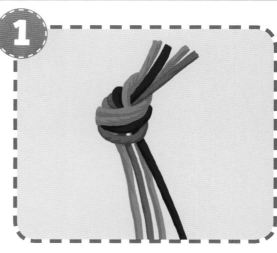

1

Take the 4 strands of cotton thread and knot them together, 8 inches from one end.

2

Thread the large bead on the bracelet and push it up as far as the knot.

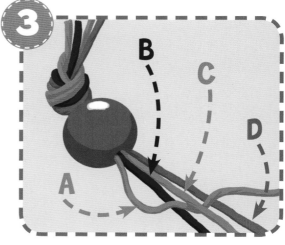

3

B   C

D

A

Spread out the 4 strands so that the 2 mauve strands are first and third from the left. Put A over B, under C, and over D. Pull A gently to tighten the weave.

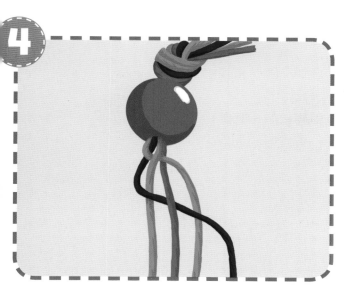

Continue weaving B over C, under D and over A, working over, under, over, under. Pull gently to tighten before starting on the next left-hand strand.

Continue weaving until you are about 3 inches from the end, then tie the knotted strands into a knot, leaving the ends loose.

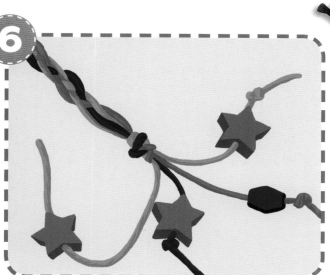

Thread a medium-sized bead onto each of the 4 loose strands and tie a knot to keep it in place.

I'm going to give my friendship bracelet to Zoe. She is coming over to my house to play. Who will you give your bracelet to?

kitty photo album

This collage photo album will make a purr-fect present for your favorite cat lover!

You will need

- 6 sheets 8½ × 11 inches, colored cardboard
- Scraps of card in orange, white, pink, green, black, and blue
- Hole punch
- Pinking shears
- White glue and brush
- 3-foot long piece of green cord

1

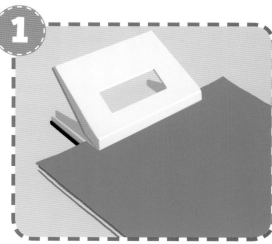

Pile together the 6 sheets of colored cardboard with the cover sheet on top. Punch 2 holes on the left-hand side.

kids 2

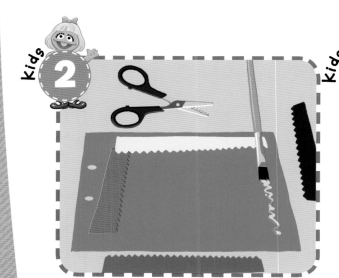

Using the pinking shears cut a strip from each of the card scraps. Arrange them to make a border on the cover and glue in place.

kids 3

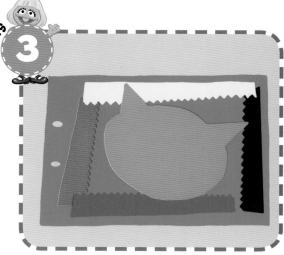

Draw and cut out a large cat face from orange cardboard. Glue it on the cover, overlapping the borders as shown.

Draw and cut out the cat's oval white eyes with green and black pupils. Cut out a pink nose, mouth, some ears, and black whiskers. Arrange these on the face and glue them in place.

Thread the length of cord through the holes, starting from the back and including all the pages. Tie in a bow at the front. Knot the ends of the cord to stop them from fraying.

Instead of an orange kitty, make a photo album with a picture of your pet on the front. Or, just make a pretty design any way you wish!

Secret book box

A secret is something that you keep to yourself. Keep your secrets safe in this special box—it looks just like a book!

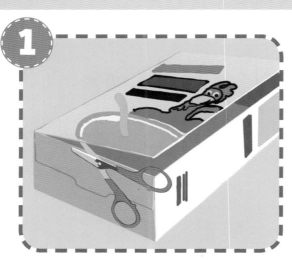

1

Cut the front of the empty box around 3 sides. Leave the left side uncut so it makes a flap.

You will need

- Empty cereal box
- 8½ x 11 inches of white cardboard
- Scissors
- Pencil and ruler
- White glue and brush
- 2½-feet piece of 1 inch yellow ribbon
- 11¾ x 16½ inch sheet of light blue foam
- 8 x 11 inch sheet of dark blue foam

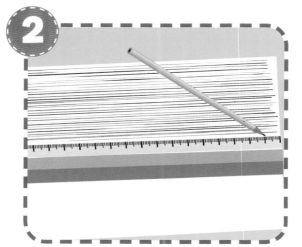

2

Using the pencil and ruler, draw straight lines on the white cardboard. Using the box as a guide, cut out 3 pieces of cardboard to fit around the sides of the box. Glue them in place.

3

Cut the ribbon in half and glue one piece to the back of the box and the other to the front flap, halfway down.

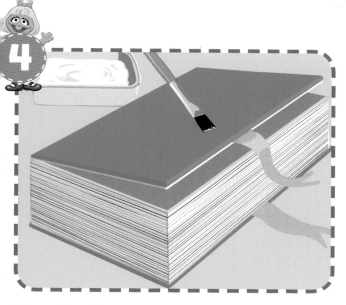

4

Using the box as a guide, cut 2 pieces of light blue foam, each a fraction of an inch bigger than the box on all sides. Glue a piece to the front flap and the other to the back.

5

Cut a piece of dark blue foam the same height as the box and ½ inch wide. Glue in place on the side of the box to make the spine of the book. Cut small pieces of foam to decorate the front and spine of the book.

You can keep anything you like in your secret book—even your Rubber Duckie!

Candy mirror

Brighten up a plain mirror with these cute candies. Or you could use beads, sequins, or buttons.

You will need

- Toothpicks and lump of modeling clay
- Bag of small soft candies
- Spray varnish
- White glue and brush
- Old mirror

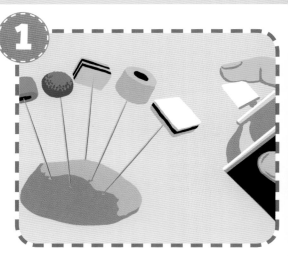

1

Press the candies onto toothpicks and push into the clay. Spray them with varnish.

kids 2

When the varnish is dry, brush glue onto the backs of the candies and stick them in a border all the way around the mirror.

BIG BIRD'S MARVELOUS MODELING

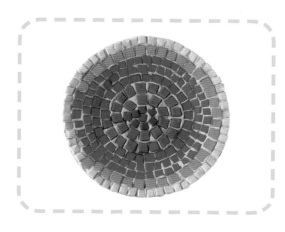

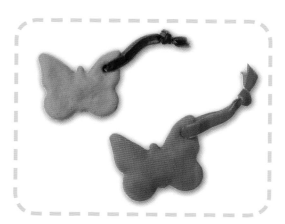

Clay eggcup

I have a great idea. Make an eggcup, then paint a funny face on your boiled egg.

You will need

- 7 ounces air-drying clay
- Plastic knife
- Egg
- Acrylic paints: blue, red, black
- Paintbrush

It's very eggs-citing!

kids **1**

Set one-quarter of the clay to one side. Roll the remaining clay into a ball and use your thumbs to work it into a bowl shape to fit the egg snugly.

3

2

Divide the remaining clay into two equal pieces. Make a fat foot shape out of each and fix them to the base of the bowl. Score the bowl with a toothpick and wet each piece to help them stick.

Turn the model the right way up and adjust the feet until the model stands flat on a surface without wobbling. Let dry overnight.

4

This looks eggs-cellent, Big Bird. Hee hee!

Paint the bowl of the eggcup and the shoes, to make an outfit.

It's turned out eggs-actly how I'd hoped. We're having fun making up words, substituting the word "egg" in them. Can you think of any more?

Mosaic plate

Granny Bird told me that a mosaic is a picture made from small pieces of material. Use clay to create a spiral like this one.

You will need

- Old dinner plate
- Oven-bake clay: white, orange, red, green, blue
- Plaster of Paris
- Butter knife
- Rolling pin
- Plate-hanging hook

Kids

1

Roll out each color of clay to about ¼ inch thick.

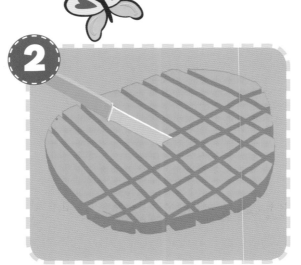

2

Cut all the clay layers into ¼ inch squares. Put the squares in the oven and bake them according to the manufacturer's instructions.

3

Mix some plaster of Paris with water in a plastic bowl and smear it all over the plate. Lay out the tiles on a work surface in a spiral pattern.

4

Add the tiles, one color at a time, pushing them into the plaster. Let dry overnight.

You can hang your plate on the wall for everyone to admire. It's so magical.

Oh me so proud! This plate is good enough to eat cookies from!

Brilliant beads

These beads are made from 3 different colors of clay, but if you only have 1 or 2 colors, simply make the beads and, when they are dry, paint them if you wish.

1

Roll the 3 colors of clay into sausage shapes and put them side by side. Using a plastic knife, cut sections of about the same size through all 3 lengths together.

kids

2

Take a section and roll it into a ball between your palms until the colors are mixed together. Repeat until you have made about 15 balls.

You will need

- Air-drying clay: green, yellow, turquoise
- Plastic knife
- 15 toothpicks
- Mug or glass
- Darning needle
- Thin elastic thread
- Scissors

Push a toothpick through the middle of each ball. Balance the sticks across the top of a mug or glass, so that the beads are fully exposed to the air, and leave them to dry. They will be ready in about 24 hours.

Using a darning needle, thread the beads onto thin elastic until you have enough to go around your wrist comfortably. Knot the 2 ends of elastic together and trim the ends.

These square beads are just as easy to make as the round ones. Make little clay balls, then gently flatten each ball on each side between your thumb and forefinger until you have little cubes.

119

Salt-dough basket

If you don't have any clay, you can create your own! Salt dough is inexpensive and easy to make and can be used for all kinds of modeling projects.

You will need

- Salt dough recipe
- Flour
- Rolling pin and plastic knife
- Aluminum foil
- Shallow, round ovenproof dish
- Old ballpoint pen or pencil
- Acrylic paints: blue, red, green and brush
- Small scrap of green felt
- Scissors
- All-purpose glue

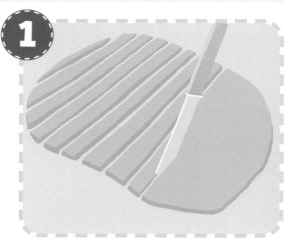

1

Shape an apple-sized ball of the dough and set aside. Sprinkle flour on the salt dough and roll it out to about ¾ inch thick. Using a plastic knife, cut 15 strips.

2

Cover the inside of the dish with aluminum foil. Lay a line of strips across the bowl. Now weave a strip down the middle of the bowl in the opposite direction.

3

Weave more strips to make the basket. Roll the last strip into a thin sausage and press around the rim. Make strawberries from the leftover dough, then poke holes in them with an old pen.

Bake the basket and strawberries in the oven according to the instructions at the start of this book. When they are cold, separate the dish from the basket. Paint the basket any color you wish and paint the strawberries red with green dots.

Cut leaf shapes from the green felt and glue them to the tops of the strawberries. Then glue the strawberries to the edge of the basket.

You can keep anything you like in your basket. I'm going to keep my favorite fruit, bananas, in mine. What's your favorite fruit?

Mini farmyard

Make your own farmyard scene of cute sheep and clucking chickens with oven-drying clay. Ask an adult to help you bake them.

kids 1

For the hens' bodies, roll and shape the brown clay into simple crescent shapes.

You will need

- Oven-bake clay: brown, red, yellow, white, black, green

Elmo found out that if you wet the edges of the clay pieces a little bit, they stick together better.

2

Roll a small lump of red clay and press it flat with your thumb. Stick it to one end of the body. Add a small yellow cone shape for the beak. Add a small red blob underneath for the wattle.

kids 3

Add tiny black blobs of clay for eyes. Make a small ball from the green clay and flatten the bottom. Place the hen on top and push it down firmly to stick it in place.

For the sheep, mold a ball of white clay into an oval shape for the body. Make a head, 2 ears, and 4 legs out of the black clay.

Stick the head, ears, and legs to the sheep's body. Bake all the animals in the oven, following the manufacturer's instructions.

These animals live on a farm. Grouches prefer living in trash cans though.

CD holder

Granola bar boxes are perfect to make this groovy CD holder, so get munching!

You will need

- 4 identical empty cardboard granola bar boxes
- Scissors
- White glue
- Masking tape
- Thick cardboard
- Torn newspaper pieces
- Paints: white, silver
- Brush
- 3 old CDs

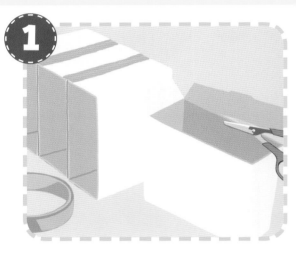

1

Cut the lids off of all the boxes. Glue the boxes in a row and add masking tape along the joins.

2

Cut out two squares of thick cardboard the same size as the box sides, and glue one to each end of the boxes.

3

Make papier-mâché mix following the recipe at the start of this book. Apply a layer of newspaper all over the outside and around the edges of the boxes.

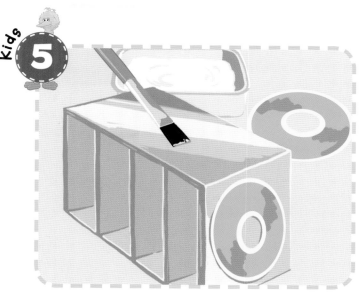

When the papier-mâché is dry, paint the boxes white all over. Let dry.

Then paint the outside silver. When it is dry, glue a CD on each end and on the top. Then fill it with your favorite music.

Elmo loves listening to music. Elmo also loves recycling old things into new toys!

Papier-mâché bowl

Balloons are great for making bowls. After the papier-mâché dries, just pop the balloon to leave a perfect bowl shape!

You will need

- Balloon
- Torn newspaper strips
- White glue, brush and water
- Scissors
- Masking tape
- Round plastic lid
- White latex paint and brush
- Ruler and pencil
- Set of acrylic paints
- Water-based varnish and brush

kids 1

Blow up the balloon. Make the papier-mâché from the recipe at the start of this book. Glue papier-mâché strips halfway up the balloon. Repeat with 3 layers.

2

When the papier-mâché is dry, pop the balloon and remove it. Trim the edges of the bowl by cutting around the rim until it's smooth and even.

kids 3

Sit the bowl in the plastic lid and tape them together. Paste 2 more layers of papier-mâché over the whole model and let dry.

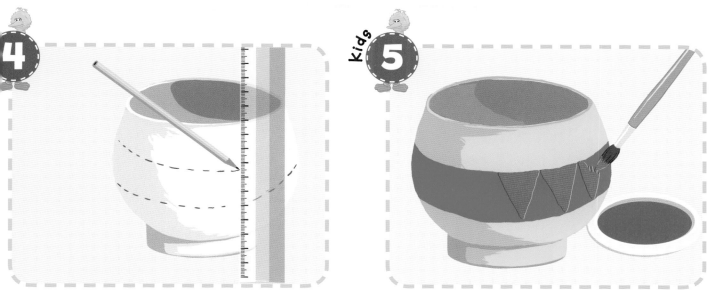

Paint the bowl all over, including the inside, with a coat of white latex paint. Let dry. Hold the ruler beside the bowl and mark 2 straight lines of dots around the bowl. Join the dots to make lines.

Paint on a striped pattern in bright colors and let dry. Add spots, triangles, or other designs. Let dry, then add a thin coat of varnish to make the bowl tough and shiny.

It's important to let the papier-mâché dry completely before you pop the balloon or start painting. If it is still soft and damp, you could easily put your finger through it and that would ruin your bowl!

Photo-frame magnet

This fridge magnet frame is designed to look like a dog's collar. It's perfect for showing off a photo of your favorite pup!

You will need

- Oven-bake clay: red, yellow
- Pencil
- White glue and brush
- Large magnet
- $8\frac{1}{4} \times 5\frac{7}{8}$ piece of thin cardboard
- Photo of your favorite dog or pet

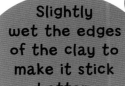

Slightly wet the edges of the clay to make it stick better.

1 Roll a piece of red clay into a sausage shape about ¾ inch thick and 4 inches long. Make the shape into a circle, overlap the edges and press them together.

2 Make a buckle and name tag from the yellow clay. Press gently to the circle. Use a pencil to make holes as shown. Put the shape on a cookie sheet and bake according to the packet's instructions.

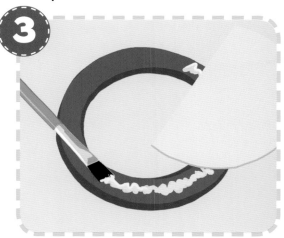

3 Cut a circle of thin cardboard slightly smaller than the frame. Cut off the top third of the circle. Brush glue onto the back of the frame and glue the cardboard to it to make a pocket.

Trim your dog photo so that it will fit easily in the frame. Slide it into the pocket.

Glue the magnet onto the back of the cardboard and let dry.

Design a frame and put a picture of yourself in it. Now all you need to do is to give it to someone who loves to see your smiling face.

Slithery snail pots

These smiling snails look great and they can store a special surprise. You can hide your tiny treasures under their shell!

kids

1

Roll a ¾-inch ball and 2 tiny balls from half of the clay. Stick the 2 tiny balls onto the larger ball. Cut 2 short pieces of pipe cleaner and push them into the larger ball.

2

With the rest of the clay from the first half, make a tapered oval shape. Use your thumbs to create an indent in the middle. Stick the head to the untapered end.

3

Roll the other half of clay into a ball and shape into a hollow shell shape. Check it fits the base of your model. Add a spiral on each side using the toothpick. Let dry overnight.

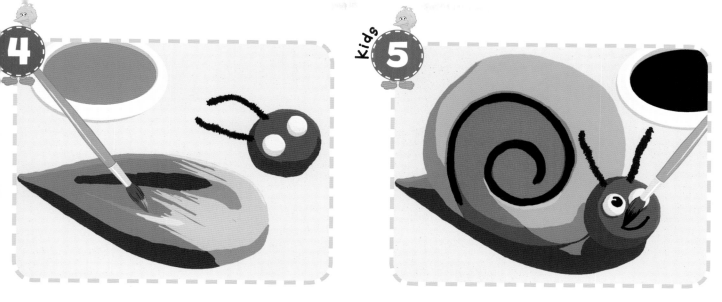

Paint the the head, the eyes, and the base any color you like.

Paint the shell and outline the spiral. Add a smiling mouth and paint on pupils for the eyes.

What super treasures will you keep inside your secret snail?

For a grasshopper pot, make a long base and lid and push 6 green pipe-cleaner legs into the base. Paint the pot bright green all over and add red spots.

Scented hangings

Hang these fragrant little butterflies in your clothes chest or closet and your clothing will always smell fresh. They make great gifts, too!

You will need

- Salt-dough mixture
- Rolling pin
- Butterfly-shaped cookie cutter
- Toothpick
- Ribbon
- Baking sheet
- Acrylic paint and paintbrushes
- Lavender essential oil

1

Make the salt dough, using the recipe at the start of the book. Roll it out to a thickness of about ¾ inch.

2 Kids

Using a cookie cutter, cut shapes out of the dough. Make a hole at the top of each shape with the toothpick.

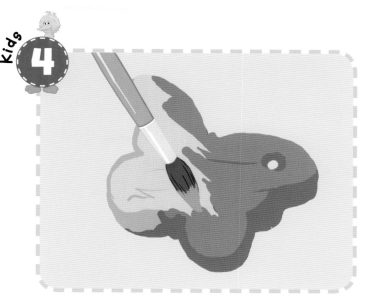

Put the shapes on a cookie sheet and bake in a pre-heated oven at 250°F for about 3 hours. Let cool.

Paint the shapes, leaving a small square on the back unpainted.

My mommy told me that lavender oil helps people to feel relaxed, so hang a butterfly over your bed. You'll soon be having sweet dreams!

Add a few drops of lavender essential oil to the unpainted area. Thread a ribbon through the hole and knot it at the back.

Heart-shaped hangings make a great Valentine's day gift for a special friend!

Sheriff's badge

Make some salt dough, then model yourself a lawman's badge, and flash it if you dare and run those bad guys out of town!

You will need

- ½ recipe salt dough
- Star-shaped cookie cutter
- Cookie sheet, greased
- Silver paint and brush
- Brooch backs
- All-purpose glue

kids 1

Roll out the dough to about ¼ inch thick. Cut out some star shapes with the cookie cutter and put them onto a greased cookie sheet.

I'm Telly and my badge shows I'm a triangle expert. What does your badge say about you?

kids 2

Make as many tiny balls as your star has points. Wet the corners of the stars and stick a ball on each corner. Bake according to the recipe at the start of the book. Paint the star silver and let dry. Glue a brooch back to the star.

SNUFFY'S TOYS & GAMES

Funky monkeys

This pair of acrobatic monkeys love just hanging around with each other! They are made from bendy pipe cleaners and fluffy pom-poms.

You will need

- 3 x 12-inch brown pipe cleaners
- White glue and brush
- 2 x 4-inch pom-poms
- 2 x 1-inch pom-poms
- Scrap of beige felt
- Black felt-tip pen
- 4 tiny wobbly eyes

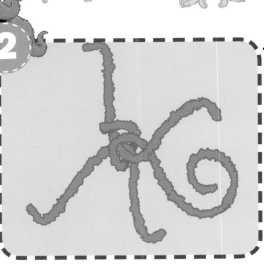

1

Cut the pipe cleaners in half to make 6 equal pieces. Bend 1 piece in half to make the legs. Bend at the ends to make feet. Repeat for the arms and hands.

kids 2

Place the arms upside down on top of the legs. Wind another piece of pipe cleaner once around the join to fix them together. Curl the end to make a tail.

kids 3

Glue 2 of the larger pom-poms together, sandwiching the legs, arms, and tail between them.

To make the head, cut a small figure-eight shape from the felt. Glue wobbly eyes to the felt face and use the pen to add nostrils and a mouth. Glue the face to a 1 inch pom-pom. Let dry.

Glue the head to the top of the pom-pom body and let dry. Bend the arms, legs, and tail into shape so it will stand up. Repeat to make the second monkey.

Creepy crawly

This terrifying tarantula is made from 4 pipe cleaners for legs, with 2 pom-poms holding them in place. Add eyes, antennas, and a hungry mouth and it'll give your friends the shivers!

Shoe-box aquarium

Make your own under-sea scene, complete with a chest full of sunken treasures. The best thing about these fish is they don't need feeding!

You will need

- 1 empty shoe box
- Acrylic paints and brush
- Scissors
- Blue acetate film cut to the same size as shoe box
- Clear adhesive tape
- White paper and pencil
- Clear thread
- Tissue paper: light and dark green

1 Cut the bottom out of the shoe box, leaving a ¾-inch border all around the edges.

kids

2 Stand the box upright and paint the outside light blue all over. When dry, paint some light green and dark blue streaks over it. Paint the inside floor sandy yellow.

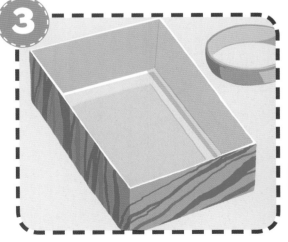

3 Cut the blue acetate film to fit inside the box. Stick it in place with tape.

On white paper, draw and color in with paint a few fish, a starfish, and a treasure chest on a big mound of brown sand. Make sure the mound is big enough to fold over and be used to stand the chest upright. Cut them out.

Using clear adhesive tape, attach clear thread to the fish. Tape the other ends of the thread to the inside top of the box, so the fish look as if they are swimming.

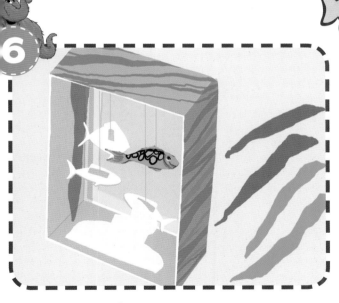

Cut 4 strips from the tissue paper and tape them to the top of the box so they hang down like seaweed. Tape the starfish to the side of the box. Fold over the bottom of the treasure chest and tape the flap to the floor so it stands up on its own.

Elmo is pretending he is swimming in the ocean. What creatures will Elmo see there?

Bottle-top snake

Use the tops of plastic soda bottles to make a super, slithery snake. Ask an adult to save you the two wine corks you need.

You will need

- Champagne-style cork
- Wine cork
- Green acrylic paint and brush
- Plastic bottle tops: 30 green, a few red and white
- Old ballpoint pen
- 3 small screw eyes
- 24-inch piece of string
- Small bell
- 2 wobbly eyes
- Scrap of red felt
- Scissors
- White glue and brush

kids

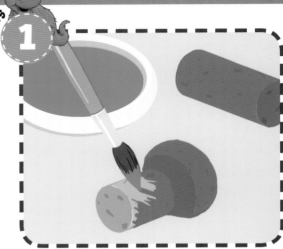

Paint both corks all over with the green acrylic paint. Let dry.

Using the old ballpoint pen, make a hole in the middle of each of the bottle tops.

Screw one eye into the top of the champagne cork. Add the bell to another screw eye, and screw this and the remaining eye into each end of the wine cork.

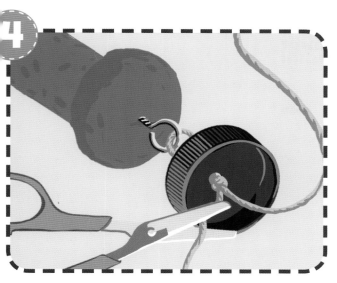

4

Thread one end of the string through the bottom of a green bottle top. Now thread it through the champagne cork's screw eye and back through the bottle top. Make a knot and trim one end only.

5

Thread all the bottle tops onto the string, keeping them all facing the same way around. Finish by tying the string to the screw eye on the wine cork.

6

Glue the wobbly eyes in place. Cut a thin forked tongue from the red felt and use the pen to poke it into the cork.

Snakes use their tongues to "taste" the air. This tells them if food is nearby. Snakes can be dangerous so if you see one, go and tell a grown-up right away and don't touch!

Bottle skittles

Play skittles in the backyard or, if it's raining, indoors. Roll a ball at the skittles and try to knock as many over as you can.

You will need

- 6 identical clear plastic drinks bottles with lids
- Ready-mixed paints: red, yellow, green
- Dishwashing liquid
- Old jug
- Self-adhesive star and planet stickers
- Funnel
- Sand
- Ball

1

In an old jug, mix the green paint with water until it looks like soup. Add a small squirt of dishwashing liquid.

kids 2

Pour some paint mixture into a bottle and put the top on. Shake the bottle to spread the paint all over the inside of the bottle. Add more paint if you need to.

kids 3

Remove the top, pour out any remaining paint and let the bottle dry. Repeat for the other bottles, making three red, two green, and one yellow skittles.

Put the funnel in the neck of the bottle and pour in sand until half full. This makes the skittles harder to knock over. Repeat for each of the bottles.

Put the tops back tightly on the bottles. Decorate the skittles with self-adhesive stickers.

Painting the skittles from the inside of the bottle means the paint won't chip when you play with them.

Fishing game

Challenge your friends to a game of magnetic fishing and see who can land the best catch!

You will need

- Sheets of white paper
- Pencil and scissors
- Acrylic paints and brush
- Aluminum foil
- Thick cardboard
- Sheet of blue cardboard
- Clear adhesive tape
- Paperclips
- 2 garden stakes and string
- 2 large, thin magnets
- White glue and brush
- Hole punch

1 Draw a fish, a crab, and a seahorse. Cut them out and draw around them to make four fish, four crabs, and two seahorses in total.

kids

2 Using bright-colored paints decorate the creatures and add eyes to the seahorses and fish. Glue colored paper onto the fish to make fins.

3 Cut one 14-inch diameter circle of cardboard and one of foil and glue them together. Cut a strip of blue cardboard about 1½ x 43 inches long and tape the ends together to make the rim of the pool.

4

Write the following numbers on the bottoms of the creatures: 2 on the fish; 5 on the crabs; and 10 on the seahorses. Slip a paperclip onto each creature.

5

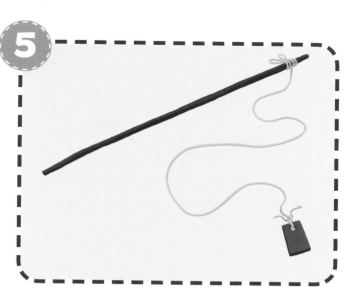

Tie one end of the string to the garden stake. Use the hole punch to make a hole in one end of the magnet. Push the string through the hole and tie a knot.

How to play

Put all the creatures in the pool and take turns to fish them out. Once they're all caught, add up the numbers on the bottoms. The winner is the person with the highest score!

Travel Checkers

This miniature game of checkers in a box is a great way to keep you and your friends from getting bored on long car or train trips.

1

Cut around the bottom of the shoe box to make a tray about 2 inches deep.

2 kids

Paint the lid and the tray red all over. You might need to do several coats to cover all the lettering. Let dry.

3

Measure the width of the tray and cut your paper into a square the same size. Draw a grid on the paper of 8 x 8 squares.

Make a grid exactly the same size on the blue paper. Cut out the blue squares and stick them onto the white grid, so that alternate squares are blue.

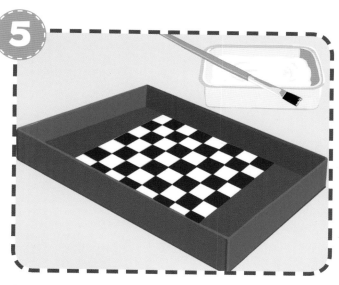

Spread white glue on the back of the paper and stick it down inside the box.

Roll each piece of clay into a sausage shape and use the plastic knife to slice each one into 12 counters. Bake them according to the manufacturer's instructions.

There are so many things to count on long journeys—trucks, cars, trees, and clouds. Can you think of other things to count when you are traveling?

Cardboard car

Vroom! This car has wheels, so it will whizz along a smooth surface. You can use the cardboard from an empty cereal box to make the body of the car.

You will need

- Sheet of cardboard
- Scissors
- Masking tape
- Papier-mâché mix
- Old newspaper
- Sandpaper
- Acrylic paints and paintbrush
- 4 plastic bottle tops
- 2 straws
- 2 wooden toothpicks
- Ruler and pencil

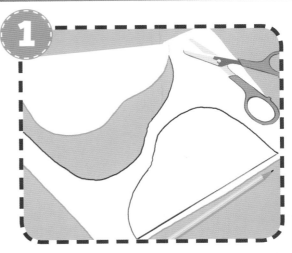

1

Use the template to trace two side-views of the car. Cut them out. Then cut out a rectangle 5-inches wide and 17 inches long for the roof.

2

Measure 2 inches in from the ends of each of the car sides. Snip out small "V"shapes. This is where the wheels will sit.

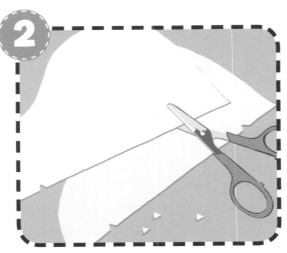

3

Tape the sides and the roof together. Cut a rectangle to fit the base of the car and tape it to the sides.

4

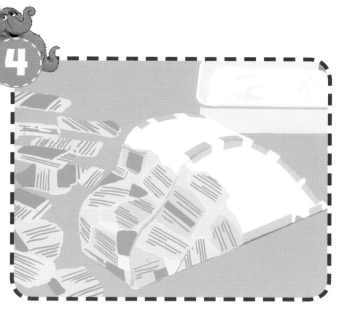

Tear up the newspaper into small pieces. Mix up some papier-mâché mix. Cover the car in two layers of papier-mâché. Let dry.

5

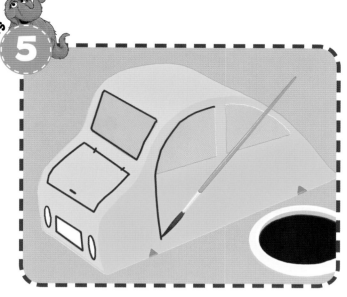

Rub the model all over with sandpaper. Paint your car yellow, then add windows, doors, a license plate, headlights, a driver, and some passengers.

Traveling by car is so much faster than pogo stick—but not as much fun!

6

For the wheels, carefully make a hole in each bottle top with the scissors. Push a straw through the hole and fix it with a small piece of toothpick. Push the straw through to the other side, trim it to fit, and add the other wheel. Repeat for the back wheels.

Bean bags

These felt bean bags are quick and easy to make, leaving you plenty of time to practice your juggling skills. You'll soon be a juggling genius!

You will need

- 3 felt rectangles of 3 x 6 inches
- White glue and brush
- Scissors
- Small dried beans (e.g. mung beans) or lentils
- Spoon
- Pom-poms: 4 yellow, 8 red
- Red and yellow thread and needle

kids **1**

Take each felt rectangle and spread glue along one of the longer edges and along one of the shorter edges. Fold it in half and let the glue dry.

kids **2**

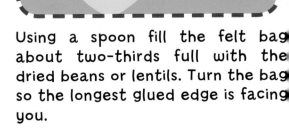

Using a spoon fill the felt bag about two-thirds full with the dried beans or lentils. Turn the bag so the longest glued edge is facing you.

My mommy made my bean bags extra-strong by sewing around the seam of each bag after I glued it. You can do that, too!

3

Brush glue inside the top of the bag and press the edges together to make the pyramid shape. Let dry.

4

Using the needle and thread, sew a pom-pom onto each of the four corners of the juggling balls.

Royal crown

This crown is fit for a king or queen! You can be the ruler of your own special kingdom!

You will need

- 8 x 11 inch tracing paper and pencil
- Strip of gold cardboard 5 x 24 inches
- Scissors, white glue and brush
- Hologram film 1 x 24 inches
- 2 strips of gold cardboard: 1½ x 13 inches
- Paperclips and paper fastener
- Purple felt
- Dinner plate
- Cotton batting
- Black acrylic paint and fine brush
- Assorted colored gems

1

Trace the the crown template. Transfer it onto the back of the gold cardboard, then repeat, butting the second section up to the first. Cut out the whole strip.

kids

2

Glue the hologram film along the base, then glue gems along the top. Glue the two ends so the crown fits loosely on your head. Hold in place with paperclips. Let dry.

3

Push a paper fastener through where the strips meet.

Mark halfway between the shapes with the pencil. Glue the gold strips to the inside of the band where these marks are. Hold in place with paperclips. Let dry.

Trace around the dinner plate and cut out a circle of purple felt. Make small snips all around the outside of the felt circle. Glue the felt to the inner brim, gluing bit by bit along the clipped edge. Let dry.

Cut a strip of cotton batting about 2 inches wide. Glue it along the bottom edge of the crown. Paint black spots about 1 inch apart along the length of the cotton batting.

A furry, cute, blue monster like myself looks even cuter in a crown.

Miniature theater

Make a shoe-box theater and get your friends to help you put on shows of your favorite stories or funny tales.

1

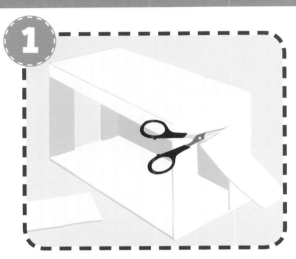

Turn the box lengthways and cut a window in each side.

2

Draw a nature scene on the back and sides. Color the scene with paints.

3

kids

Cut two pieces of red fabric 8 x 16 inches. Glue them to the front of the box and decorate with gold ribbon. Cut a strip of red fabric 31 inches long, and cut one edge into a scalloped shape. Glue it along the top.

Draw a picture of Goldilocks and the Three Bears onto thick white paper. Paint them and let dry.

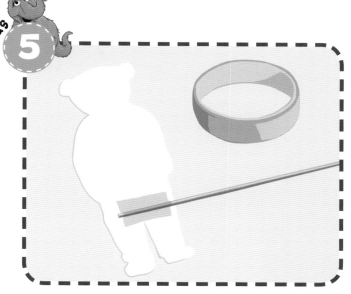

Cut out the characters and tape a wooden skewer to the back of each, near their feet.

6

Make a table by cutting into a small square box. Draw a blue checked tablecloth, cut it out, and glue it to the table. Draw three porridge bowls and cut them out, leaving small tabs to stick them to the table.

Elmo is ready to put on his show for Baby David! You can choose any of your favorite characters to put in your show.

Tabletop soccer

If you've got plenty of puff, try a game of blow soccer. You can only move the ball by blowing through the straw—no hands allowed!

1

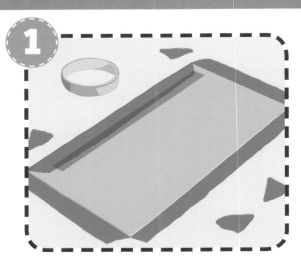

Cover the cardboard with the green felt, pull it tight, and tape it at the back.

You will need

- Sheet of cardboard, 20 x 28 inches
- Green felt 28 x 35 inches
- Clear adhesive tape
- Wood glue
- Wood batons: 2 x 28 inches, 2 x 20 inches
- Acrylic paints: yellow, white
- Scissors
- Small cardboard box
- Red paper
- 4 toothpicks
- Drinking straws and ping-pong ball

2

You can use chalk for the lines, but you'll have to redraw the lines because it wears off quickly.

kids

3

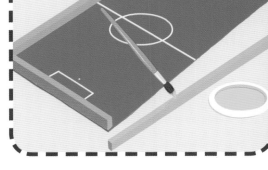

Turn it over and draw soccer field markings lightly in pencil. Paint over the lines in white.

Paint the wood batons yellow and glue them together to make a fence around the field.

4

Cut a small cardbord box in half to make goals.

5

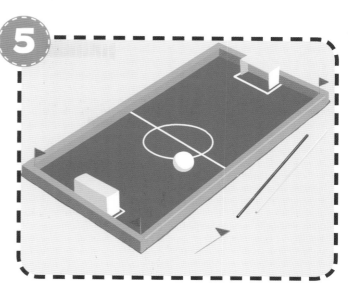

Put the goals inside the white boxes on the field. Cut out four small paper triangles and glue them to toothpicks to make corner flags.

Elmo likes playing soccer. It's hard to move the ball without using Elmo's hands, but Elmo tries!

Tic-tac-toe game

Be green and save paper by making a tic-tac-toe game you can use over and over again!

You will need

- Foam: 1 sheet each in black, orange, purple, and green
- Sheet of thick cardboard 8 x 8 inches
- Ruler
- Scissors
- White glue and brush
- Paper and pencil

1

Cut an 8 x 8 inch square of black foam and glue it to the sheet of thick cardboard.

2

Use the ruler and pencil to draw four strips on the orange foam, 8 inches long and about ¼ inch wide. Cut them out.

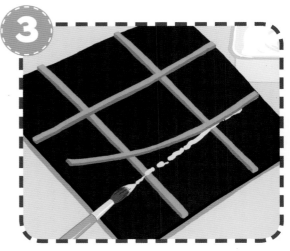

3

Glue the four strips of orange foam to the black foam in a crisscross shape. You can use the ruler to help you position them evenly.

Cut the green funky foam in half and glue the halves together to make a double-thick sheet. Repeat with the purple foam.

Draw a large "X" and an "O" onto the paper. Cut the shapes out and trace them onto the foam. Make five green "Xs" and five purple "Os". Cut out the shapes, and you're ready to play!

Instead of making your Os and Xs, you could also use seashells or buttons to play with. Have fun counting them. Heh, heh, heh.

Pickup sticks

To win this game you'll need a steady hand and nerves of steel. Be careful though—one false move and you'll be out!

1

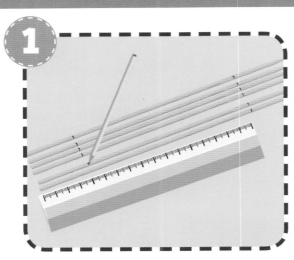

Line up six sticks in a row. Use a pencil and ruler to mark each stick 1½ inches from each end.

kids

2

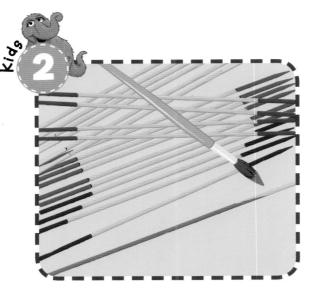

Paint the ends of the six sticks red up to the marks you made. Make orange, green, and blue sets in the same way. Paint the last stick purple all over.

You will need

- 25 wooden sticks
- Acrylic paints: red, orange, green, blue, purple
- Thin paintbrush
- Ruler and pencil

How to play

Drop all the sticks except the purple one in a random heap. Each player takes a turn to try to remove sticks from the pile, one by one, using the purple stick to help. You must only touch the stick you are aiming for—move any others and your turn is over! The player who removes the most sticks is the winner.

GROVER'S CELEBRATION CRAFTS

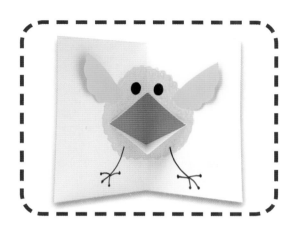

Spring chick card

Baby chicks are fuzzy and small, and make peeping sounds with their beaks. Celebrate Spring by making this chick card for someone you love.

You will need

✦ 8 x 11 inch sheet of white cardboard
✦ 8 x 11 inch sheet of orange cardboard
✦ Scissors
✦ Gluestick
✦ Pencil
✦ Felt-tip pens or colored pencils
✦ Sheet of yellow paper

1 Fold both sheets of cardboard in half. Cut a 2¼-inch slit in the white card in the center of the folded sheet, at right angles to the fold.

2 Carefully fold in both edges of the slit and make creases so that when you open and close the card, a beak shape pops out.

3 Draw a large, round chick's body around the beak shape. Use scribbly strokes to make your chick look fluffy. Color in the beak.

4

Draw black eyes and legs on the body. Cut two wing shapes from the yellow paper and glue them to the body. Make sure the wings stay inside the edges of the card.

5

Paste glue over the back of the white card, avoiding the beak part. Stick it to the orange card, and write a special message on the front of the card.

Now you can give your friends and family their very own birdy buddy!

Chinese dragon

Dragons are symbols of good fortune in Chinese New Year celebrations. Maybe this colorful dragon puppet will bring you luck, so keep your fingers crossed!

You will need

- 8 x 11 inch colored paper: red, yellow, green
- Scissors
- White glue and brush
- Clear adhesive tape
- Tissue paper: pink and white
- Pencil
- Paints: black, red, yellow, gold, white
- Paintbrush
- Thick white paper
- 2 garden stakes

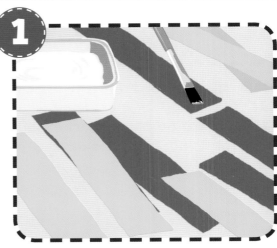

1 Cut the red and yellow paper into 1½-inch wide strips. Glue all the red strips together to make a strip about 47 inches long. Repeat with the yellow strips.

2 Glue one end of the two long strips together at right angles to each other. Fold one strip over the other, and press down. Repeat until the whole strip is folded.

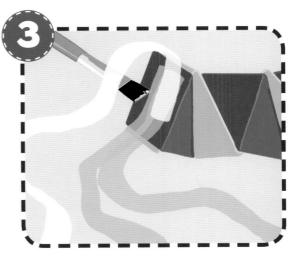

3 Cut strips of pink and white tissue paper and glue them to one end of the strip for a tail.

4

5

Draw a dragon's head onto thick white paper. Cut it out and paint it yellow or orange with a red mouth. Leave the eye and teeth unpainted.

Add an eye, two nostrils, and black lips. Paint gold highlights on the face. Make 2 fringes by snipping into the yellow and green paper and glue to the back of the head. Add strips of pink tissue to the forehead.

6

Use clear adhesive tape to attach a garden stake to the back of the dragon's head. Tape another near the tail and your dragon puppet is ready to roar!

Me can also add sequins or shiny candy wrappers to dragon's eye and head.

Christmas crackers

Make your family laugh at Christmas. Put all your favorite jokes in these homemade Christmas crackers.

1

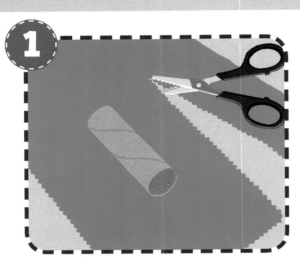

Using pinking shears, cut a piece of green crêpe paper three times as long as the toilet-paper tube and wide enough to go around it with a 1 inch overlap.

You will need

- Crêpe paper: green and red
- Cardboard toilet-paper tubes
- Pinking shears
- Jokes on small pieces of paper
- Hard candies in wrappers
- Cracker snaps
- Rubber band
- Sparkly pipe cleaners
- Self adhesive hologram tape.
- Small gift bows: red and green

Kids 2

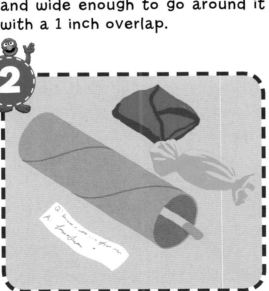

Put a wrapped candy, folded paper crown, joke and cracker snap in the toilet-paper tube.

3

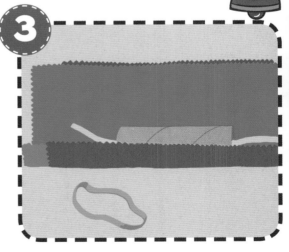

Cut red crêpe paper the same width but ¾ inch shorter than the green. Wrap both layers around the tube and hold them in place with a rubber band.

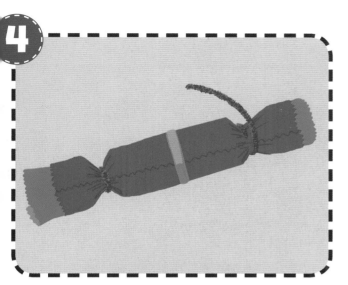

4

Cut 2 x 6 inch lengths of the pipe cleaners. Twist the ends of the paper and wrap the pipe cleaners around each end of the crackers to keep them closed.

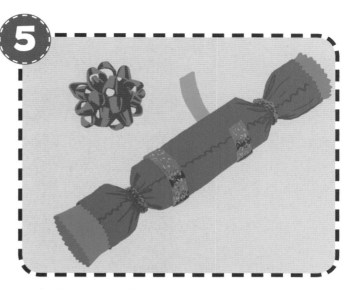

5

Cut 2 strips of hologram tape and stick them around the tube. Remove the rubber band and decorate the tube with a gift bow.

Paper crowns

It's easy to make paper crowns. Cut a piece of tissue paper about 6 x 24 inches. Glue both ends together and fold it in half twice. Cut the paper to a point. Open it out and you have a crown!

167

Halloween bat card

Before you go trick-or-treating, make a spooky bat silhouette card for a really horrid Halloween gift!

You will need

- 8 x 11 inch sheet of black cardboard
- Sheet of orange paper $4\frac{3}{4}$ x $7\frac{1}{4}$ inches
- Tracing paper and pencil
- 5 x 8 inch sheet black paper
- Scissors
- Gluestick
- 2 green sequins

kids 1

Fold the black cardboard in half. Glue the orange paper to the front of the cardboard. Make sure you leave a black border around the outside.

2

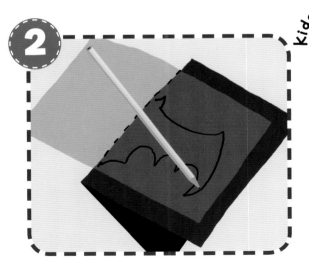

Trace the template onto tracing paper. Fold the sheet of black paper in half and put the tracing paper on top. Trace the half-bat shape onto the cardboard.

kids 3

Cut around the half-bat shape, taking care not to cut into the fold. Open out the bat shape and apply glue all over one side. Stick it to the front of the card.

Stick on green sequins using the gluestick, to add menacing bat's eyes.

I love Halloween because there are so many things to count. Pumpkins, trick-or-treaters, candy, and of course, batties. What a wonderful day to count things.

Chocolate nests

Make an Easter treat for the family with yummy chocolate nests. Don't forget to ask an adult to help.

You will need

For 5 nests:

- Heaped ½ cup sugar
- ½ cup butter
- ½ cup cocoa powder
- 2 tablespoons corn syrup
- 2½ ounces shredded wheat
- Aluminum foil
- Medium saucepan
- Wooden spoon
- Mini chocolate eggs or jelly beans

1

Put the sugar, cocoa powder, butter, and corn syrup into the saucepan.

2

Place the pan on a low heat and stir slowly until the mixture melts. Don't let it boil!

Kids 3

Let the mixture cool slightly. Crumble the shredded wheat into the mixture and stir until the shredded wheat is covered.

Make the aluminum foil into five bowl shapes. Add some mixture and press down in the middle to make nest shapes. Put them in the fridge to cool and set.

When the nests are fully set, remove the foil and fill the chocolate nests with the mini chocolate eggs.

I wonder how big these delicious chocolate nests would need to be to hold me?

Hanukkah candleholder

Jewish people celebrate Hanukkah, the Festival of Lights by lighting special candles and exchanging gifts. This Hannukah candleholder is called a menorah.

kids

1

You will need

- ☆ Tracing paper and pencil
- ☆ 18 ounces air-hardening clay
- ☆ Rolling pin
- ☆ Plastic knife
- ☆ Toothpick
- ☆ Ruler and old pen
- ☆ Gold paint and paintbrush
- ☆ 9 small candles

Roll out the clay to ¾ inch. Put the template onto the clay and cut around it. Use your toothpick to make 9 small holes in the flat end for the candles.

2

Make a mark on the pencil so you know how far down to push.

3

Next, push the end of the pencil about ½ inch into each hole. Do this for all except the middle hole which should only be ¼ inch deep, so the candle will stand taller.

Roll out a small piece of clay and cut out a star shape using the template. Attach it to one side of the candlestick by wetting and scoring both pieces of clay to help them stick.

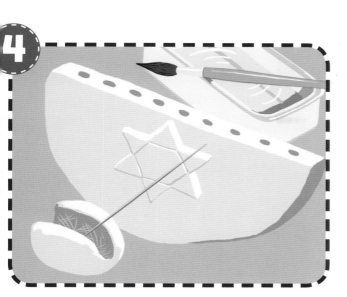

4 Roll out a 2-inch ball of clay for the stand. Flatten the bottom and make a groove along the top. Stick it to the bottom of the candlestick. Make sure it stands firmly, and leave it to dry.

Kids 5 Paint the candlestick gold all over and leave it to dry. Insert the 9 candles into the candlestick holes and ask an adult to light them.

A Hannukah menorah always has 9 candles. Eight candles represent the 8 days of Hannukah and the tallest candle, called the Helper candle, is used to light the other 8.

Snowmen card

Make these adorable cut-out Christmas cards for all your friends. They're "snow" cool!

You will need

- ✳ 8 x 11 inch sheet white cardboard
- ✳ Pencil and ruler
- ✳ Scraps of black cardboard
- ✳ Felt-tip pens
- ✳ Silver glitter
- ✳ White glue and brush

1

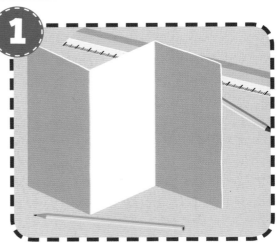

Mark the card along the long side, at 3¾ and 7¾ inches. Fold the card into three equal sections as shown above.

2

Draw a snowman shape on the card and cut it out. Be careful not to cut through the folds on the sides.

3

Open up the card. Cut 3 hats from the black cardboard and glue them on the snowmen's heads.

Use the felt-tip pens to draw eyes, mouths, and buttons. Finish with orange carroty noses, brown canes, and scarves.

Paint on a thin layer of glue and sprinkle on the silver glitter for a sparkly finishing touch.

Advent calendar

Start your countdown to Christmas with this Advent calendar. Fill the boxes with your favorite treats and enjoy a daily surprise while you wait for Christmas!

You will need

- 16 x 23 inch sheet green cardboard
- Sheet of thick white cardboard 10 x 31 inches
- 6 x 8 inch sheet red cardboard
- White glue and brush
- Scrap gold cardboard
- Pencil and rubber
- Scissors
- 23 small empty matchboxes plus one large one
- Silver and red foil gift wrap
- Gold gift ribbon cut into 20 x 24 inch pieces
- Large star sequins
- 25 hard candies or chocolates
- Gold marker pen

1

Glue the green cardboard to the center of the white cardboard, leaving space at the top and bottom. Cut a star from the gold cardboard and glue it to the top. Cut a pot shape from the red cardboard and glue it as shown.

2

Draw a large Christmas tree shape on the green cardboard and cut the whole shape out.

3

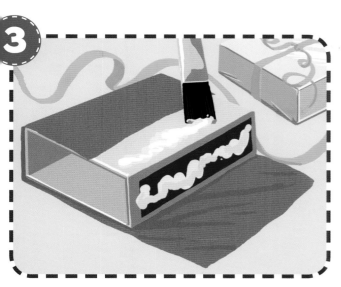

Cover 12 matchboxes in red foil paper and 12 in silver. Tie a length of gift ribbon around each matchbox and tie a double knot in it. Curl the ribbon by pinching it firmly between your thumbnail and index finger and pulling it between them.

4

Using the gold marker pen, number each of the small boxes from 1 to 23. Write "24" on the big matchbox. Put a wrapped candy or chocolate in each box, and put two in the 24 box.

5

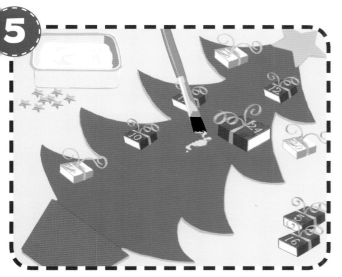

Arrange boxes 1 to 23 randomly on the Christmas tree and put the 24 box in the middle. Glue all the boxes in place. Glue sequin stars onto the tree in the gaps between the boxes.

Elmo's been a very busy monster making this advent calendar. Elmo loves getting a present every day!

Mother's Day photo booklet

Your mom will love to keep her favorite pictures of you in this super photo album.

You will need

- 2 pieces of cardboard 6 x 6 inches
- 2 sheets 8 x 11 inch purple paper
- Clear adhesive tape
- White glue and brush
- 3 feet turquoise ribbon
- Sheet of turquoise paper 6 x 24 inches
- Pencil and ruler
- Blue corrugated card 4 x 4 inches
- Small square of purple felt
- Pinking shears
- Colored gems

1

Wrap each sheet of purple paper around a square of cardboard. Fold over the edges and fix in place with clear adhesive tape.

2

Cut the ribbon into 4 equal strips. Glue to the back of the purple cards, as shown above. Trim the end of each ribbon into a "V" shape.

3

Glue the end of the sheet of turquoise paper to the back of one of the purple boards. It should cover where the ribbon is attached to the purple card.

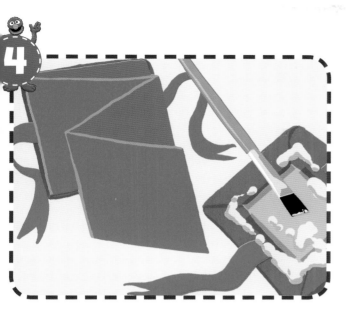

Fold the turquoise paper strip three times, accordian-style. Glue the last fold to the back of the remaining purple board.

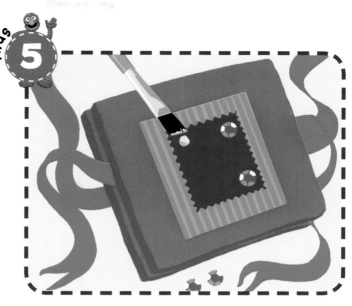

Decorate the front by sticking on some blue corrugated cardboard, then a smaller square of purple felt cut with pinking shears. Glue some gems to the felt as a finishing touch.

Cut triangles from purple felt to fix the corners of your photos in place.

Christmas stars

Are you in a hurry for Christmas? Make some sparkly foil tree decorations while you wait for the big day.

You will need

- Thick card (e.g. from a box of laundry detergent)
- Tracing paper and pencil
- Scissors
- White glue and brush
- Foil candy wrappers
- Sequin stars
- Hole punch
- Gold cord

1

Draw a star onto the tracing paper. Put the tracing on the card and draw over the lines to transfer it to the card.

2

Use the scissors to carefully cut out the star design.

3 kids

Tear the candy wrappers into small pieces. Glue the pieces all over the star, overlapping them until the whole shape is covered. Let dry.

4 Glue the sequin stars onto both sides of the foil-covered star. Let dry.

5 Use the hole punch to make a hole in one of the points of the star. Thread a length of gold cord through the hole and knot the ends together. Then hang them on the tree.

Elmo likes to help his daddy hang decorations on the Christmas tree.

Halloween lantern

Halloween would not be complete without a glowing jack-o'-lantern. Put one in your window to greet trick-or-treaters.

You will need

- ✲ Medium-sized pumpkin
- ✲ Spoon or ice-cream scoop
- ✲ Felt-tip pen
- ✲ Small knife
- ✲ Tea light

Kids 1

Scoop out the insides of the pumpkin using a spoon or an ice-cream scoop.

2

Use a felt-tip pen to draw a scary face onto the pumpkin. Or draw your favorite designs, like circles or triangles.

3

Now for the tricky part! Ask an adult to cut away the marked pattern, using a sharp knife.

4

Add a tea light and ask an adult to light it.

If your pumpkin dries out and looks withered, soak it in cold water for a few hours and it will be as good as new.

Golf paperweight

If your dad or grandfather plays golf he will love this Father's Day gift. Especially if it's made by a furry, cute, blue monster like myself.

You will need

- Wooden doorknob
- Paints: white, green, red
- Paintbrush
- Air-drying clay
- Strong wood glue

kids 1

Paint the doorknob white except for the flat top. Next paint the flat top green. Then paint little tufts of grass around the rounded bottom.

2

Roll a clay ball and make dimples all over it with the end of the brush. Paint it white. Make a tee from the clay and paint it red.

3

When the clay has hardened, glue the ball and the tee to the flat, green surface. Let dry.

ABBY CADABBY'S GARDEN CRAFTS

Fabulous flower pot

Flowers come in all shapes and sizes, and some of them smell so pretty. Make a special pot to keep your favorite bunch of flowers in.

You will need

- ✹✹ Flower-patterned gift wrap or
- ✹✹ Pictures of flowers from magazines
- ✹✹ White glue and brush
- ✹✹ Plastic flowerpot

Cut out the prettiest flower shapes from the gift wrap or magazines.

Brush glue around the outside of the plastic flowerpot.

Glue the cut-out flowers to the flowerpot. Overlap them to make a pretty pattern.

4

Brush a thin layer of glue over the cut-outs to make the pot waterproof.

You can decorate some pots with pictures of different leaves, or butterflies, or anything else you like. Elmo likes it when butterflies land on flowers. When did you last see a butterfly?

Magical watering can

Plants and flowers need sun, soil, and water. I've painted a funny face on my watering can. Why don't you give it a try, too?

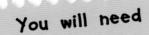

You will need

★★ Pencil
★★ Plain metal watering can
★★ Acrylic paints
★★ Paintbrushes

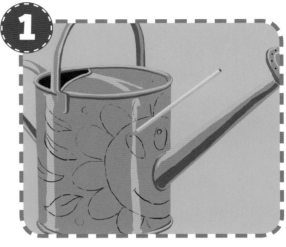

1

Make sure the watering can is clean and dry. Use a pencil to mark out a design, like this flowery face using the spout as the nose.

2 kids

Paint on the face and petals, or other designs you have created. Let dry.

3 kids

Add another coat of paint if necessary. Let dry.

4

Add patterns around the face, handles, or spout. Let dry thoroughly.

You'll love watering your flowers with this pretty can.

Egg carton pagoda

A pagoda is a tower that has lots of layers or levels placed one on top of the other. Make this pagoda scene using an empty egg carton.

You will need

★★ Shoe box lid
★★ Empty egg carton
★★ Scissors
★★ 6 small bottle caps
★★ White glue and brush
★★ Sheet of blue paper
★★ Plastic wrap
★★ Tissue paper
★★ Popsicle sticks
★★ Acrylic paints and paintbrush

kids **1**

Paint the inside and outside of a shoe box lid. Let dry. This will be the base for the garden.

kids **2**

Cut 6 sections from an old egg carton then paint 3 orange, and 3 red, inside and out.

3

Glue the sections together with a small bottle cap between each section to make a gap. Glue the pagoda onto the lid. Let dry.

4 Cut a pond shape from the blue paper. Brush glue over the paper and press down a piece of plastic wrap on top to make it look like water.

5 Scrunch up small balls of tissue paper to make trees and glue them into the garden. Use painted Popsicle sticks to make a bridge and a fence.

Add balls of tissue paper flowers to the trees, and some tissue paper fish to your pond. What other creatures could you add to your pagoda scene?

Shell jewelry box

Use seashells to make a beautiful jewelry box from an old food container. Collect shells if you live near the beach, or buy them from a craft supplier.

You will need

- ✯✯ Round food container with lid
- ✯✯ 2 squares of red felt
- ✯✯ Pencil
- ✯✯ Scissors
- ✯✯ White glue and brush
- ✯✯ Blue acrylic paint and brush
- ✯✯ Assorted seashells

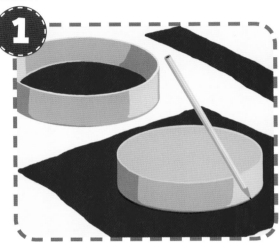

1

Draw around the lid of the box onto the red felt. Cut it out, and stick it inside the lid. Repeat, and stick onto the base of the box.

2

Measure the depth of the box and cut a long strip of felt the same width. Glue it around the inside of the box. Trim the ends to make it fit neatly. Let dry.

3

Paint the outside and base of both the lid and box with the blue acrylic paint.

4 Arrange the shells on the box lid and glue them on.

5 Smaller boxes can be decorated with a single shell. Use them as gift boxes for earrings and rings.

Seashells are the homes of creatures called shellfish. Once the animal has gone, you can use the shells for all sorts of crafts.

Twig furniture

Collect twigs from the backyard or your local park. Use them to make fun furniture, maybe for a doll's house, or for fun games.

1

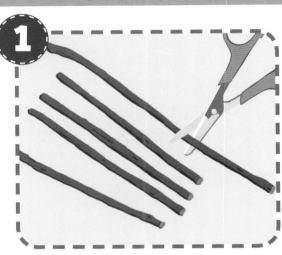

To make a chair, cut 15 thin sticks about 1½ inches long.

You will need
- About 30 thin twigs
- Scissors
- Ruler
- Wood glue and brush

2

Put 9 sticks side by side and glue 2 sticks at either end to hold them together. This will be the seat. Let dry.

3

Measure and cut 2 x 4¾ inch sticks for the back of the chair. Glue the seat halfway up the sticks. Glue 2 sticks 2¼ inches long, to the front of the seat to make front legs.

Glue 4 sticks around the bottom of the chair, and one at the top. Glue 2 sticks diagonally to the back to make a cross. Let dry.

To make the table, glue 8 sticks with a shorter stick at either end.

6

Elmo imagines characters from stories, like Goldilocks and the Three Bears, sitting in this little chair.

Glue 4 legs to the table top, then make the table sturdy by gluing 2 long and 2 short twigs to the legs, and 2 long twigs crosswise under the table.

Cactus garden

It's so easy to grow a cactus garden.
A sunny windowsill and some water once
a week are all these prickly plants need.

You will need

★ 5 small assorted cacti
★ Stone bowl large enough
   for all 5 cacti
★ Cactus soil mix
★ Wad of paper towels
★ Old spoon
★ Colored gravel or sand

kids

1

Put a thin layer of gravel in the
bottom of the bowl. Add soil mix
almost to the top of the bowl.
Make a hole in the soil mix with
your finger.

2

Fold the paper towels around the
tallest cactus and remove it from
its pot. Put it in the hole you have
made and push down the soil mix
firmly all around it.

3

Make another hole in the soil mix
and plant the second tallest cactus
in the same way as before.

Continue planting. Use an old spoon to press down the soil mix firmly around the base of each cactus.

Using the spoon, arrange the gravel around the base of each cactus until the soil mix is covered.

If you don't have colored gravel, make a desert garden instead by spreading sand on top of the soil mix.

Garden on a plate

Making a miniature garden will keep you busy on a rainy day. Collect tiny cuttings of shrubs and flowers from the backyard and get planting!

You will need

- ★ Old dinner plate
- ★ Soil mix
- ★ Moss, grass, and small flowers, e.g. daisies
- ★ Cuttings from shrubs
- ★ Fir tree twig
- ★ Aluminum foil
- ★ Old jar lid
- ★ 2 twigs and length of string
- ★ Paper and colored pencils
- ★ Scissors
- ★ Small pebbles

kids 1

Put a ¼ inch layer of soil mix on the plate. Press moss into about three-quarters of the area.

kids 2

Put small pebbles around the plate edge and make a path of pebbles in the soil, as shown.

3

Push a fir twig into the soil to make a miniature tree. Then push the flowers, shrubs, and grass into the soil.

4

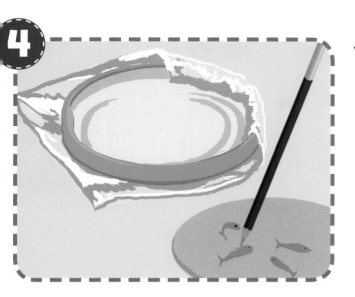

Mold aluminum foil around an old jar lid to make a pond. Cut out a paper circle to fit in the bottom of the lid. Color it blue, and draw some goldfish onto it. Put some more blades of grass around the pond to look like reeds.

Draw some clothes on a piece of white paper, giving them tags so you can hang them on the washing line. Color them and cut them out.

6

Make a washing line from the twigs and string. Hide two small pieces of plasticine in the moss and push the twigs into them. Glue the clothes to the line.

Spritz your garden with water to keep it fresh. Replace the flowers when they begin to wilt.

Pressed-flower card

Pressed flowers can be used to make beautiful greeting cards. Don't forget to check with an adult before you pick their favorite flowers!

You will need

- ★★ Flowers and leaves
- ★★ Heavy books (e.g. dictionaries)
- ★★ Paper towels
- ★★ White glue mixed with equal amount of water, and brush
- ★★ Cream cardboard 16 x 18 inches
- ★★ Scissors and ruler

kids

1

Pick some flower petals and leaves. Arrange them on paper towels, then put another piece of paper towel on top. Place them inside a book.

2

Place a pile of heavy books on top of the book with the flower, petals, and leaves inside. Leave them for at least two weeks.

3

Fold the cream cardboard in half and make a sharp crease with the point of the scissors and a ruler. Be careful not to cut the cardboard.

4

Remove the pressed petals and leaves from the book. Arrange them on the front of the card and glue them in position.

It might be hard to wait for the flowers to be ready—waiting is hard. Just think how much fun you'll have making the rest of the card when they're ready though. Can you remember another time you had to wait for something?

Bottle garden

If you'd like a garden but you don't have much room, this bottle garden is perfect. Just remember to water it once a week and your plants will be happy.

You will need

- Large glass jar with lid
- Clear adhesive tape
- Old spoon
- Cotton ball
- 2 wooden skewers
- Colored gravel
- Soil mix
- Small plants

Make your bottle garden more interesting with a tropical bird on a stick from a garden center. Now scram!

1 Start by taping the spoon to a wooden skewer, using lots of adhesive tape. This is for digging. Make a cleaning tool by taping a cotton ball to the other skewer.

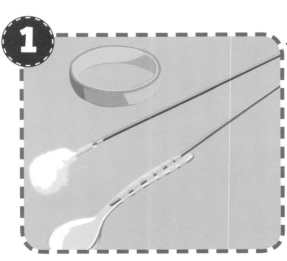

2 Spoon about 1½ inches of colored gravel into the bottom of the jar.

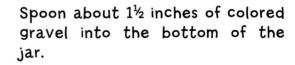

Now add about 3 inches of moist soil mix and press it down with your hands.

Use the spoon to make a hole in the soil mix. Add one of the plants and press the soil down firmly around its base. Add more plants in the same way.

Dip the cotton ball in water and squeeze it out. Use your cleaning tool to wipe away any smears of soil mix from the sides of the jar.

Flower garland

My mommy helped me make this colorful garland. It's a necklace made of flowers. It's so magic!

You will need

★★ 80 sheets of tissue paper in 2 different colors (40 of each) cut into squares of 8 × 8 inches
★★ Bag of pipe cleaners
★★ Length of elastic or ribbon
★★ Scissors

1

Stack 4 sheets of one color tissue paper together and fold over 5 times to make an accordian shape.

2

Cut both ends into a round shape then twist a pipe cleaner around the middle. Don't trim the ends of the pipe cleaner.

3

Gently separate out the tissue paper on both sides of the pipe cleaner into a flower shape.

Twist the ends of the pipe cleaner around the ribbon or elastic and make sure the ends are not sticking out. Keep adding flowers until your garland is done.

Nonny is Hawaiian. She told me that Hawaiians make flower garlands called "leis" as a sign of love and friendship.

Leaf creatures

These leaf creatures look so funny and they're easy to make. You just need some leaves and some imagination.

kids 1

Choose a large dried leaf and glue it onto the piece of cardboard.

You will need

⋆⋆ Various dried leaves
⋆⋆ Piece of cardboard (any color)
⋆⋆ White glue and brush
⋆⋆ Colored pens
⋆⋆ Colored paper
⋆⋆ Scissors
⋆⋆ Wobbly eyes, or colored dot stickers

kids 2

Choose some smaller leaves and stick them to the cardboard for hands, feet, and ears. Draw lines between the small leaves and the big leaf for arms and legs.

3

Stick wobbly eyes onto the leaf and add a smile shape cut from the colored paper.

4

Make more leaf creatures using different kinds of leaves. Make funny faces, like 3 eyes or curly antennae.

Elmo loves making leaf creatures best. Elmo is going to make up names for these leaf creatures. Do you want to try too?

Alpine rock garden

Alpines are the very small plants that can be planted in gravel or pebble gardens. They need to be outdoors because they usually grow on mountain slopes.

You will need
- Alpine plants
- Plastic plant container
- Pebbles or stones
- Sand
- Trowel
- Gravel mix

Put some pebbles in the bottom of the container and use the trowel to fill it half way with sand.

Leave the plants in their pots and arrange them on top of the sand. Then add some more sand around the pots to hold them in place.

Place a thick layer of gravel over the sand and the pots but leave the plants sticking out of the top. Put some pebbles or stones on top of the gravel.

4

Water the gravel regularly to keep the plants moist.

Wow! This rocky garden looks beautiful.

Potpourri bag

This pretty scented bag is also called a "sachet." If you place it in your drawer, it will keep your clothes smelling sweet like flowers.

You will need

★ Tray
★ Lavender flowers
★ Rose petals
★ Thin fabric 4 x 12 inches
★ Fabric glue
★ Rubber band
★ Colored ribbon
★ Scissors
★ Colored felt or fabric scraps
★ Beads or sequins (optional)

1

Spread out the lavender flowers and rose petals on a tray and allow them to dry for a couple of weeks.

2

Glue along the long sides of the fabric. Fold in half to make a bag. Press the edges together. Let dry.

3

Place some of the dried flowers inside the bag and gather the top together with a rubber band, then tie the ribbon on top.

4

Cut out small shapes from fabric or felt and glue them onto the bag. Glue on beads or sequins for extra decoration.

That smells too sweet for Grouches! I'd much rather smell garbage!

Mini grass house

Grow your own miniature grass house. It's so simple and fun too. Then make up a story about your house!

You will need

- 4 thin kitchen sponges
- Scissors
- Felt-tip pen
- Clear plastic cake box with lid (about 6-inches deep)
- Water
- Grass seed
- Straight sewing pins

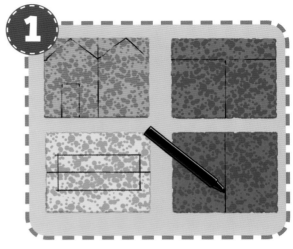

1 Mark out the sponges as above. Cut to make the roof, walls, and yard for the house.

2 Assemble the sides of the house inside the plastic lid. Fix these with straight sewing pins to make them more secure.

3 Dampen the roof and yard sponges with water, then place them in position in the container lid as shown.

4

Sprinkle grass seed onto the roof and yard. Put the clear part of the cake box over your house to cover it. Moisten the sponges occasionally so they don't dry out, and watch your grass grow!

Hola! The word "casa" means "house" in Spanish. Draw a picture of your house or casa on a piece of plain paper.

Flowery basket

Baskets are great for carrying things. Make yours super-special by adding a pretty flower pattern.

You will need

★★ Pencil
★★ 2 different-sized round lids (4-inches in diameter and 2-inches in diameter)
★★ 5 sheets of colored paper: pink, orange, blue, purple and yellow
★★ Scissors
★★ White glue and brush
★★ Colored ribbon (1 yard)
★★ Small plain basket

1

Using the pencil draw around the circular lids onto different sheets of colored paper. Cut out the circles.

2

Fold the circles in half, then in half again. Draw 3 petals onto the paper.

3

Cut around the petal outlines and open out the flowers. Stick the smaller petal shape onto the larger one with glue. Cut a small circle and stick it in the middle.

4

Wind a ribbon around the outside of the basket and the handle. Glue the ends together to fix the ribbon in place. Glue the flowers onto the ribbon.

This basket has colorful flowers on the outside. What will you choose to put inside your basket?

Shell plant pot

The next time you're at the beach, pick up a handful of seashells, or ask your mommy to buy some at a craft store. They make a plain plant pot magic!

You will need

★★ Seashells
★★ Acrylic paint
★★ Paintbrushes
★★ Clean plant pot (plastic or ceramic)
★★ White glue and brush

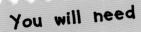

kids 1

Paint some shells in bright colors. Let dry. Paint leaves on the side of a plant pot. Let dry.

kids 2

Glue the shells onto the plant pot. Let the glue dry.

3

Paint snail bodies coming out from under the shells, or create other designs you like around the shells and on the pot.

4 Paint faces and antennae onto the snails, or add other patterns. Let dry. Now add a plant to your pot.

Elmo loves going to the beach and feeling the water splash across his feet! What kind of creatures can you find in the sea?

Bottle top vase

Use an old plastic bottle to make a colorful vase to keep beautiful flowers in. Reusing things helps keep the Earth clean!

You will need

★★ Several (20–30) plastic bottle caps
★★ Acrylic paint
★★ Paintbrushes
★★ Big plastic bottle
★★ Scissors
★★ Old newspaper
★★ White glue and brush

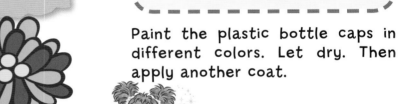

1 Paint the plastic bottle caps in different colors. Let dry. Then apply another coat.

2 Cut a clean, empty plastic bottle in half, crosswise.

3 Push some scrunched up newspaper inside the bottle to help support it while you glue the caps onto the bottle.

218

4

Brush glue on the bottle tops, then stick them around the side of the bottle.

I love making new things out of other people's garbage. Some people call it "recycling," but it's always wonderful trash to me!

Pretty plant labels

If you have lots of plants in pots in your garden, you can use these cute tags to help you remember their names. Plants and flowers are so magical!

You will need

- Felt-tip pen
- Colored craft foam
- Scissors
- Pipe cleaners
- White glue and brush
- Wobbly eyes
- Popsicle sticks

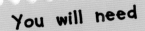

1

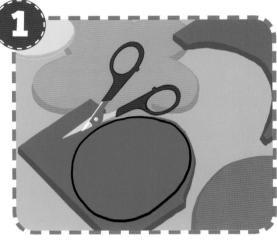

With a felt-tip pen, draw some simple shapes, such as a ladybug, a flower, or a tomato on pieces of colored craft foam. Cut them out.

2

Use smaller foam shapes or pipe cleaners to create butterfly antennae or ladybug legs. Glue in place and let dry.

3

Glue on some wobbly eyes, if you wish; let dry. Glue each shape onto a Popsicle stick.

4

SWEET PEA

TOMATO

SWEET PEA

Push your labels into plant pots, seed trays or your garden. Ask an adult to write the name of the plant on the label.

Did you know that tomatoes are actually fruit not vegetables? What's your favorite fruit?

DAFFODIL

TOMATO

Templates

Trace these shapes onto another piece of paper or card before you cut them out.

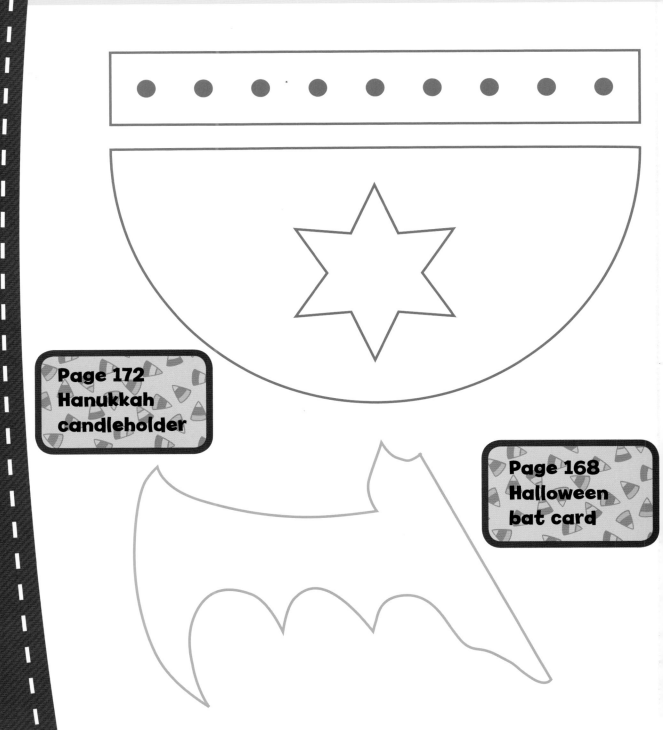

Page 172
Hanukkah candleholder

Page 168
Halloween bat card

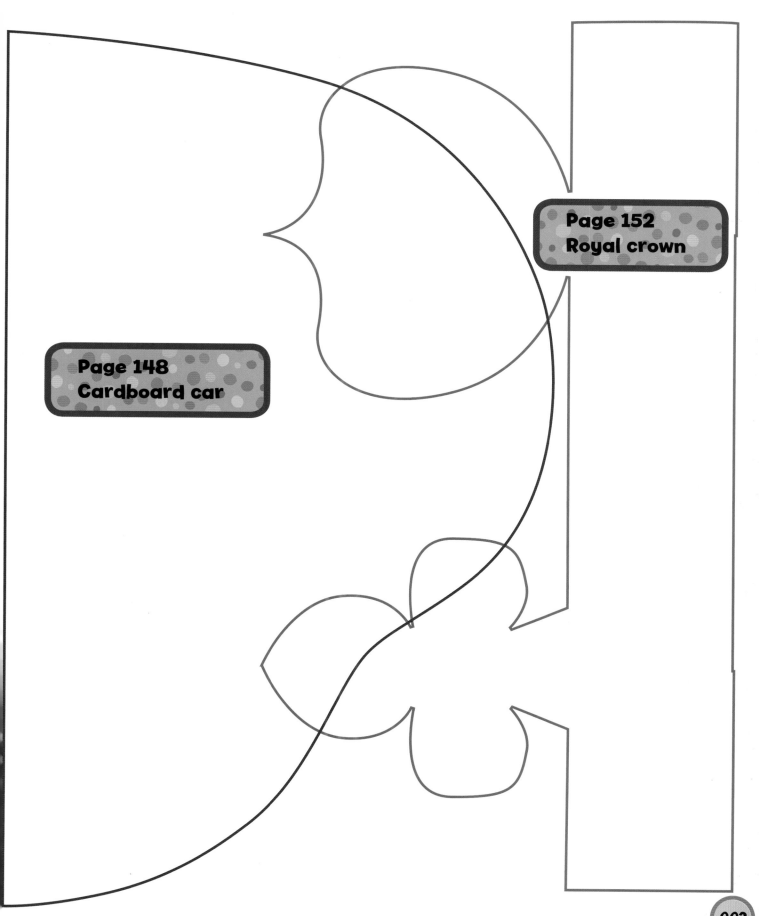

Page 152
Royal crown

Page 148
Cardboard car

Index